Americashire

Americashire

A Field Guide to a Marriage

Jennifer Richardson

SHE WRITES PRESS

Published 2013
Printed in the United States of America
ISBN: 978-1-938314-30-8
Library of Congress Control Number: 2013930841

For information, address:
She Writes Press
1563 Solano Ave #546
Berkeley, CA 94707

Author's Note:

I have changed the names of most but not all individuals in this book, and
there are several composite characters. I have also changed the location of
one event. While none of these changes impact the substance of the story, I
hope they provide a modicum of anonymity to the innocent occupants of the
Cotswolds, all of whom I am inordinately fond of.

Contents

Part One: Weekender

Pink Foil Strips

SPRING IN THE COTSWOLDS happens very slowly and all at once. In exchange for a few cheerful daffodils, the British collectively suspend their disbelief and start to talk of it in March. But spring doesn't really happen until mid-April on a particular day, when the landscape is dun brown in the morning but by evening you find that green has tipped the balance. Soon lush shag piles of minty-green grass and weeds and shoots and blooms line the country lanes, rising into pea-soup hedgerows, then the brown latticework of trees still bare except for pinch-faced buds. Over the next two weeks, these unwind into a canopy of chartreuse lace, set off by a sprinkling of bluebells on the woodland floor. These are not blue, lavender, lilac, or violet. They are plain purple, the one you get in the Crayola eight-pack.

Rapeseed happens next. Nothing changes the landscape of the Cotswolds more drastically or quickly than the en masse bloom of this flower. It is the color of Ronald McDonald's jumpsuit or the cheap mustard you get in a plastic packet with your corndog at the beach, a color that should not occur in nature, yet it does. It appears in swathes that render the hills a crude patchwork of yellow and green and drives half the population crazy with its hay-fever-provoking scent. Despite all this, I love it. I love everything about this brash landscape of unrepentant lime greens and artificial-food-coloring yellows, which is why I start to feel anxious about its demise almost as soon as I notice it's happening. Soon May blossom whites and peachy cones of horse-chestnut blooms

will be sneaking onto the perimeter, silently upstaging their rau-
cous counterparts with understated elegance. The Cotswolds of
Matisse will slip into the diffused light of the Cotswolds of Monet.

Amidst the ephemeral pleasures of spring in the countryside,
there was something else to be anxious about. It was wrapped up in
a rectangular pink foil strip with twenty-eight pills sealed inside.
There were six of those strips to be exact, one for each month of
the renewed birth control prescription I had just picked up from
the village pharmacy. For the past few months, my husband, D,
and I had studiously avoided speaking any further about the "big
talk" we had given to my parents over Christmas in which we had
announced I was going to try to get pregnant. To be fair, there was
plenty to be distracted by in our new country life. But the truth
was my ambivalence toward motherhood had not shifted, despite
large quantities of fresh air.

The pink foil-wrapped revelation of my ambivalence shook my
husband. A long-held tenet of our relationship was that I was the
decisive one, the one who could be counted on to just get on with
it. I presided over the world of black and white, the left-brained,
the rational. D held court in the domain of the emotional, the
intuitive, the creative. He cries in movies; I bring the tissues. He
rearranges the furniture; I pay the mortgage on time. In short, my
prescription refill was an act of war: I was invading his territory,
and he was pissed.

But before I go any further let me explain how I, a then-thirty-
six-year-old American, ended up contemplating motherhood in a
Cotswold village with a population dwarfed by that of any single
London street. The stock explanation is that we needed to get a
good night's sleep. Since moving to England from Los Angeles,
my British husband and I had failed to find accommodation
conducive to this simple aim. Our first flat was on a Bayswater
side street filled with tall white stucco-fronted terraces that had
once been grand single-family homes. They had long since been
divided and subdivided again into a rabbit warren of hundreds
of studio and one-bedroom flats. D had secured ours online

ahead of our arrival in London, and I'll never forget the feeling of shock upon climbing the four narrow flights of stairs, my arms laden with bursting suitcases, and flinging open the door for the first time to behold just how small three hundred ninety-six square feet really is. Despite its size and thanks to its Kensington Gardens–adjacent address, it cost more in rent each month than the mortgage payment on the Los Angeles home we had just left behind. As if that wasn't enough, the pipes knocked all night and a chorus of lunatics routinely serenaded us, their howls ricocheting off the urban canyon formed by the back-to-back mansion blocks.

More recently, we had been living in a stretch of West London that had failed to live up to the promise of gentrification implicit in its Notting Hill–adjacent location. This flat was on the first floor of a three-story brick Victorian terrace, which meant we had upstairs neighbors. Their day seemed to start when ours was finishing, and, other than the possibility they were hosting a midnight furniture-rearrangement league, I never came up with a better explanation for the frequent guests stomping up and down the stairs at odd hours than that our neighbor was a drug dealer.

There were other compromises associated with living in central London if, as ours was, your housing budget was limited to a scant quarter million. You might need to live on a street where you occasionally see a man relieving himself behind the dumpsters on the corner or be neighbors with a house full of squatters on the premises of a former Conservative Club, sign and irony still intact. You might wonder what that lady in a miniskirt and a cropped fur coat is doing talking to that gentleman when you leave the house for an early morning jog, or, just once, be greeted by a large yellow sign asking if you know anything about the body dumped in the canal as you decide it's best to upgrade your jog to a sprint along the towpath. And if you're young enough, you can probably dismiss these kinds of things as quirky and colorful, the very fiber of your bohemian urban life. But we were old enough to realize that D's recent modest inheritance—enough to give us some additional square-footage in our current London neighborhood, but not to deliver us into the genteel reaches of, say, Kensington and Chelsea—was well spent on a cottage in the country, if only for weekends. And the truth was we were both partial to the idea of a weekend house.

Weekend house. It had a certain ring to it that was pleasing to the pretensions of our middle-class ears. Nobody had a weekend home where I grew up in Florida, presumably because we all already lived near the beach. The only people I had ever heard of with weekend homes were New Yorkers fleeing to the Hamptons, which seemed suitably glamorous. D grew up in Liverpool in a middle-class home turned working class by his father's penchant for drinking his salary. In that universe, a weekend home in the country was beyond imagination. And so we chose it, a recently flooded, two-hundred-year-old cottage without central heating, ninety miles away from London where we worked and lived. There was lots of time to change our minds while the place was drying out, but just before Christmas that year we spent our first night in our very own rural idyll.

A House with a Name

Our country house came with a name, Drovers Cottage, spelled out in gold ye-olde-English script on a black plaque hanging above the front door. I had no idea what Drovers meant, but, being American, I was a sucker for a house with a name. I loved it regardless.

Some Googling revealed a drover to be one who drives livestock long distances to market. I assumed this had something to do with the sheep trade that made the Cotswolds rich, but the cottage postdates the height of the town's golden fleece-fuelled glory. Further Googling revealed a connection that matched the age of the cottage. Welsh cattle drovers are documented to have used a route through our town in the nineteenth century. Opposite our cottage are Stable and Hayloft Cottages, which was all I needed to corroborate my bucolic narrative.

The cottage is humble, bearing no resemblance to the grandeur implied by the phrase "country house." I prefer to think of it as a small yet perfectly formed expression of its terroir, two narrow stories built from the ubiquitous local honey-hued stone and terraced snugly between an identical neighbor on one end and a larger, three-story version of itself on the other. Its back garden in its current pebbled state could not support a pair of chickens, much less the sheep the Cotswolds are known for, although I did meet a woman who had once lived in the house and managed to keep a pony in the shed. The row of cottages curves around in a boomerang shape, ending in a stream and the mill, one of the two the town history describes as part of this pre-Norman hamlet. Here the lane is lined with trees whose branches entwine overhead like an entrance to a fairy tale.

Behind the mill is the most distinctive architectural feature of the town, the twelfth-century church that came into its own with fifteenth-century wool money. If a docent is on hand when you visit, he or she will be sure to highlight the collection of brasses in the likenesses of the wealthy who originally built the church, but I was most impressed by the Disney-Haunted-Mansion-style assortment of ancient gravestones. There's also a tower crowned by a gleaming cockerel weathervane. It's home to the eight-bell carillon that rings to the tune of "Hanover" every hour through the day and night. This is what you notice on your first overnight visit, although we've grown accustomed to it, only really noticing the bells when they ring at length for a wedding or a christening or when we are actually trying to tell the time. It is far more pleasurable, if slightly riskier, to lie in bed and try to determine if you should get up by counting the strokes of the church bell rather than being jolted into consciousness by the bleating of a cell-phone alarm.

At the opposite end of our row of cottages is the entrance to the village green, now a small parking lot bordered by well-kept stone and half-timbered buildings. Other than the fact that the green has been paved over, this is the part of town that has the kind of shops that play along with my American notion of what English village commerce should entail. This includes a butcher that sells Eastleach Spotless sausages, made from pigs in our sister village farther along the River Leach, and a small art gallery and framing shop owned by a local artist. At the bottom of the green lays the town's only museum, specializing in the suitably obscure wonders of mechanical music, and a small shopfront selling very large dollhouses. A mile farther along this route will take you to the main A road, and on to Oxford and London.

In the other direction, past the war memorial permanently decorated with a poppy wreath, is the West End, which sufficiently distinguishes itself from London's theater neighborhood of the same name with a higgledy-piggledy row of Georgian and medieval houses. At the end of the End are the Roman road and the old Victorian prison, now a coffee shop and Internet café and home to the village's only ATM. If it weren't for its high-walled garden—the former prison yard—with its display of gypsy caravans and occasional outdoor Shakespeare performance, I might be less charmed.

The market square anchors the town. The market held here each Wednesday is a legacy from the early thirteenth century when King Henry III granted the town a charter that allowed it, but is less quaint than you would imagine. For every vendor selling homemade jams there is another selling the same selection of cut-rate household items you find at any Dollar Store. The square is blissfully free of the shopfronts that mark most town centers in England, rendering them virtually indistinguishable from one another: no Boots, Marks and Spencer, Halfords, Vodafone, Prêt a Manger, or Dixons. There is, however, a Londis, which is something like a 7-Eleven minus the Slurpees and plus a selection of Cotswold postcards. It has been sympathetically branded as The Cotswold Store. There's also a pub, a pharmacy, a post office, a green grocer and bakery, a takeout Chinese restaurant, and a wine bar, these last two having figured unreasonably in our decision to buy here.

The local wine bar is a hub for the neighboring villages. The downstairs space has beamed ceilings strung with fairy lights and an open fireplace opposite the bar. For our first few months in the Cotswolds, we would sit quietly on a Friday night at the big wooden table at the front of the room, observing from a distance the elbow-patched and tweed-wearing band of locals who hovered at the back bar and trying to pluck up the courage to barge through them to order. Eventually, at the hands of these patrons, D and I would receive a rural education worthy of the Royal Agricultural College, our local Oxbridge of farming. But it was the long-serving barman, Roddy, who first took us under his wing in a warm, if somewhat alcoholic, twist on the welcome wagon.

Roddy had worked at the wine bar for years, a sort of postre-tirement diversion for him. He wears a checkered shirt with an apron when he is behind the bar, adding a leather waistcoat and a woolen flat cap when he is off-duty. He has a thick head of wavy, dark hair and rosy cheeks and has been spotted on occasion wearing a cravat. A self-described Zionist Anglo-Catholic, his favorite topic of conversation was the idiocy of our then-Labour prime minister. He also loves talking to me about American politics and the time he spent working in Chicago and the agricultural belt of California, stories he repeats many nights without causing me any annoyance. On paper, he is not a likely candidate for a friend, being far too close to an eccentric British version of my Ronald Reagan-loving, lapsed-Catholic father. Yet he is one of my favorite people precisely because of all his quirks, proving that leniency and acceptance are given far more rein outside the bounds of family. That said, it was the bounds of family that had brought us to England in the first place.

Fairs and Fêtes

ON THE FACE OF IT, there had been a lot of reasons we had left Los Angeles for London, most of which belonged to my husband. It had started several years before we actually made the move, on September 11, 2001. Although we did not lose anyone we knew, we, like many others, were marked by the events of that day. For D, a Brit who had been living in Los Angeles for over eight years at the time, the attack brought up a sense of not feeling safe in America. This country was not his home because such terrible things would not happen in the country he called home. It was irrational of course—five years earlier the IRA had bombed the city center of Manchester, England—but it was how he felt. Then, three years after September 11, 2001, on the same evening that George Bush was reelected president, D's best friend went to sleep and didn't wake up. He died at thirty-nine of an undiagnosed heart condition. But the tipping point was when D's brother called from England to let us know their mother was too ill to continue living alone. Not long after, D started sniffing around for a job in the old country.

I was enjoying my life in Los Angeles and, while I was sympathetic to his mother's health, I had no wish to up sticks for London. Supremely confident I had set a condition that was both perfectly reasonable in outward appearance and totally unachievable, I cavalierly told D I would go if he got a job that would fund our move. My smugness got its comeuppance swiftly, and in the spring of 2005, I found myself beholding the grandeur of that three-hundred-ninety-six-square-foot flat in Bayswater, West London.

By the time we arrived, my mother-in-law had been moved into a nursing home near her home in the northwest of England. For nothing else than to spend more time with her, our move to England had been warranted—her health soon went into free fall. During this time, we were spending most weekends driving up and down the M6 from London to Lancaster where she was in the hospital, which is how we developed a taste for the Costwolds. It was something of a midpoint on the journey, and dinner in a country pub there would inevitably turn into an inquiry about a room for the evening. Indulging in a fantasy of buying a second home in our new favorite place became our distraction from the death that was playing out in front of us. The feverish pace of viewings of these potential rural retreats and an impetuous string of unreasonable offers, all mercifully rebuffed, gave it away.

Before long this morphed into our suspicion that we were second-home-hunting in the Cotswolds in lieu of facing the reality of our relationship, most often voiced in the midst of a flaming fight as something like, "Our marriage is fucked. We have no right to buy a second home; we can't even get along." (It was unnecessary to state the obvious: If our fitness as second-homeowners was in question, then our fitness to be parents was a moot point.) Yet we plodded on, making an offer that was accepted on Drovers Cottage.

The friction came to a head a few months before we were supposed to close on the deal, during a weekend visit for the town's summer fair, an event we were told was not to be missed. It also helped that it fell on the same weekend as the Notting Hill Carnival, a street party that takes place each August bank-holiday weekend in the eponymous London neighborhood. The first year we lived in London I convinced D we should stay in town to experience the festivities from the prime view of the balcony of our flat, which was right on the main parade route. That most of our neighbors had boarded up their houses and left town should have been a hint of what was to come. After being repeatedly accosted by parade goers demanding to use our bathroom, then being kept awake until 2:00 AM on Tuesday morning while sound systems from stray floats shook the doorframes of our basement bedroom, I learned my lesson. (I told you getting a good night's sleep in London was hard.) So when our Cotswold town announced their fair would take place on the August bank-holiday weekend, it took no convincing for us to attend this fine example of the British summer tradition of fêtes and fairs and shows.

By British summer fête standards, our town fair is elaborate. There are the requisite tea and cake stands, a handful of carnival rides, and a fire truck. And then there are the competitions, the rules of which are spelled out in great detail in a hand-stapled brochure featuring a clip-art fruit and vegetable basket. I was as excited over this brochure as I would have been if it were an engraved invitation for a weekend with Charlie and Camilla at their Highgrove estate. I reviewed the rules and conditions of entry, which are very serious indeed:

1. All entries to be submitted between 10:00 AM and 12:00 PM and to remain on show until 4:30 PM.

2. No competitor may win more than ONE PRIZE in any class.

3. The judge's decision is FINAL.

4. Horticulture and cookery entries not claimed by 4:45 PM deemed to have been given to the Village Hall will be auctioned at 5:15 PM.

5. Any protest must be made in writing, and the committee will reallocate prizes accordingly, if the protest is upheld.

6. The committee, while taking ordinary care, will not be responsible for any loss or damage to exhibits.

7. All exhibits shall have been made or grown by the exhibitor.

8. The winners of the challenge cups MUST undertake to return them to the chairman at least two weeks before the annual show.

Ever since I got the brochure I had been dreaming of entering something in the cookery section, maybe a Victoria sponge or brown loaf. But a word from a kindly village lady, our soon-to-be-neighbor, prevented me from getting up the courage to do so.

"Best to stay out of village politics," she had murmured, when I inquired, which, although I didn't understand it at the time, was good advice.

The horticultural section of the show is hosted in the village hall, and a local offers to give me a guided tour. For each plate of "six perfect shallots," he provides careful details of village provenance. There are speckled eggs, apples, pears, plums, runner beans, cauliflower, and cabbage. Glossy red onions the size of babies' heads wear decorative green ties around their tops. Enormous marrows and elaborate vegetable boxes in categories like "collection of six kinds of homegrown vegetables in a box not larger than two-foot square" dominate the far wall. Rows of brilliant dahlias (large, medium, pom-pom, cactus), asters, and gladiola run the length of the hall.

Inside the church are the cookery, craft, flower arrangement, junior, teenage, and photographic section entries. I take mental note of the items I want to bid on in the upcoming auction, coveting a child's cap knitted to resemble a Christmas pudding, homemade wines, lemon curd, pickled onions, and Bakewell tarts, my favorite dessert.

At 5:15 PM sharp, the auction begins. Here Roddy trades in his bar apron to provide his services as a rather capable auctioneer.

He hoists armfuls of giant leeks in the air, spawning a collective intake of breath at both the grandeur and the smell. He invades the personal space of competing bidders, egging them on at pace: "C'mon lady, c'mon, it's a fantastic marmalade, award winning, not another one of these to be found." The crowd loves it. In no time, people have worked themselves into a frenzy worthy of a Damien Hirst on the block at Sotheby's. A successful bid on the second-place winner in the "Homemade Wine: Dry" category yields me a bottle labeled "Parsip and Ginge." I assume this means parsnip and ginger, an understandable mistake if the winemaker penned the label after consuming some of his or her own wares. Six shortbread biscuits and a box of tomatoes later, I engage in a fierce battle for a Bakewell tart. The bidding and my desperation escalate in step until D gallantly intercedes with a decisive bid of £5. Murmurs of "outsider" are heard around the hall, but I don't care. I am still high from the spectacle. When it was all over, we owned a trio of leeks, a baffling quantity of red onions, and a box of fancy Thornton's mints that D won in the raffle.

We had worked up a hunger from all that bidding and so headed over to the playing field where the local cricket team was holding a barbecue. D and I were standing in line waiting to order when it happened. He turned to me to demand something. I don't remember what, another hamburger perhaps? What I do remember is that his mouth was still full with his first hamburger, and his contempt was both perfect and complete as he barked his order at me. My high spirits from the auction evaporated. I headed for the drinks tent to buy a beer and give myself some mental cool-down space. I was furious about the way he had spoken to me, much less in public.

Like the best spousal spats, this one had pressed all my childhood hot buttons about my father ranting at my mother. In two seconds, I was back in my Florida tract house, in the swimming pool with my childhood friend, Patti Stephenson. As my father's shouting boomed out the louvered windows of his den onto the patio, I bobbed furiously, mortified, willing him to shut up and acknowledging nothing to Patti.

Back at the summer fair, D and I spent the next half hour on various machinations over cell phones. (Given the size and reception of the town, we would have been served just as well by two cups on a string.) This culminated in a declaration from D that we were leaving, a well-worn party trick of his. It works like this: When he's mad at me, he threatens not to do something I want to do or to leave somewhere he knows that I want to stay. I get hooked, never mind the fact that by the time this happens the situation has invariably become so unpleasant that any person in his right mind would also want to go.

Once in the car headed for London, it was D's turn to have his childhood hot buttons pressed. I was screaming and spitting and morphing before his very eyes into his schizophrenic mother wielding an ax on the hood of his father's car. (Personally I think that's a reasonable tactic for a wife and mother to engage in to try to prevent her alcoholic husband from going to the pub for the seventh consecutive night, but that's another story.)

Where both D and I differ from our parents is our ability to back down from a fight almost as quickly as we got there. It took about thirty miles before we had a tearful reconciliation at a Tesco gas station on the A40. We turned the car around and made it back to the summer fair in time to see six black Labradors performing synchronized stunts in St. George's field.

Divorce was by then out of the question; it would be too embarrassing to have to tell people I left my husband for talking to me with his mouth full. Having children, however, was still very much in question. If we couldn't even make it through a drama-free afternoon at a country fair, how would we ever cope with a child? It was a question that would have to wait. For the time being our marriage had survived, and soon we would be the proud owners of a cottage no more than a hundred meters away from where gun dogs had performed tricks on a summer's day.

Irish Nachos

NOT LONG AFTER WE CLOSED on the cottage, we returned to the United States for Christmas vacation with my family. This is how we went from sitting in a cozy Cotswold pub one evening to a booth at an Irish theme pub in suburban southwest Florida with my parents the next. Why my father chose to take two British residents known for their liberal use of sarcasm to a mock Irish pub in Florida is beside the point, although not beside the point enough for me to notice that the menu included authentic Irish nachos.

The purpose of the evening out was to tell my parents that D and I were going to try to get pregnant in the new year. This is a loaded topic with my parents, who have yet to be made grandparents by my sister or me. (I gave them a dog, but this doesn't seem to count.) My sister, my only sibling, was at that point single and had just turned forty. In my parents' book, this amounted to a write-off in the grandchildren stakes. I was their only hope, and at two months shy of thirty-six, a source of considerable anxiety. So far they had only been able to stand by and watch as my friends and cousins produced offspring at an alarming rate. That Christmas alone, two of my girlfriends had new babies to introduce. A third had lost patience with acupuncture and diet and had moved onto hard fertility drugs.

By previous arrangement, the task of breaking the news fell to D. Shortly into our first pints of some red Irish beer that doesn't actually exist in Ireland, he informed my parents that we had some news we'd like to share with them.

Now these are not the kinds of conversations I have with my parents. We are not a sharing type of family, and each of us reacted to D's overture with our own brand of awkwardness. I shrank into the booth, focusing on the newly intriguing shiny surface of my beer glass. My mother's eyes widened and her head wobbled, no doubt anticipating the news that I was already pregnant and wondering why I was still drinking beer. My father remained stock-still except for a minor facial adjustment to assemble a politely inquisitive face. I don't remember exactly what D said, probably because I was holding my breath and nearing blackout at the time, but it was over quickly, and I knew he had told them because my mother was welling up, and my father was beaming like an idiot.

My mother then informed us she had it all figured out: This cottage-in-the-country thing was part of settling down and having kids—better schools, fresh air, an altogether nicer place to grow up. She got it. My father waited a few beats then inquired what I thought of all this. To his credit, he had noticed that following D's proclamation I resembled a deer in headlights. My mother, on the other hand, had transitioned into full-blown whimpering sobs and was not going to let a little thing like perceptiveness of my feelings ruin her moment of glory.

"I feel… fine about it," I said slowly, trying but failing to muster a more enthusiastic adjective, one that wouldn't betray my true feelings as a reluctant potential new-mother-to-be.

And then the food arrived—chips and curry—delivering my family and me from the uncomfortable intimacy that had so nearly descended upon us.

I was glad I had resisted D's suggestion for a more dramatic delivery of the news that I was going to try to get pregnant. On the flight from London to Miami, he had tried to convince me that we should write it down on a piece of paper, then wrap it up in box after box, like Russian nesting dolls, and present it to my parents on Christmas morning. I balked at the idea, mostly because I knew that with that kind of buildup my parents would be expecting the real thing—an actual pregnancy—not just some crappy intention to have a lot of sex without birth control in the new year. Best to avoid that kind of disappointment on Christmas day, as my father was prone to overreact, a trait he later demonstrated with a spectacular tantrum over the blandness of the Christmas dinner stuffing.

I had agreed to the considerably more low-key "big talk" format to break the news, only because D had persisted that we needed to tell them. Why he was so eager to communicate this information was a mystery to me. He only sees my parents once a year, so maybe he just wanted to capitalize on a rare chance for son-in-law kudos. It still didn't explain his determination. After all, this is a man who calls children "spawn" and parents "breeders." He's good with babies—he chalks this up to his googly eyes—but his distaste for adolescents is well voiced, progressing into outright disdain for teenagers.

In the year before our marriage we almost split up over the topic of children. He didn't want to have any. I wasn't sure, but wanted the option open. The debate reached a crescendo in a group therapy session, as these things do when you are a resident of Los Angeles, which we were at the time. I was ready to break the engagement, and he backed down. The marriage was the most important thing to him, with or without a child involved.

In our early married years, the topic of children was a nonissue. D continued to be vocal about his desire not to have any, and I was still youngish and in no particular hurry. Then, on the brink of thirty-five, I started to mentally prep him for the possibility. When we eventually bought a flat in London—the one with the midnight furniture-rearrangement league upstairs—I insisted on the place that had a second bedroom. It was a broom closet of a second bedroom, but, I thought, a crib can fit in a broom closet. I dropped comments about my great maternity-leave benefits— and they really are great compared to the United States—into casual conversation. I made mental calculations about when would be the best time to get pregnant to take full advantage of those benefits: "must have been an employee for two years by the time you reach fifteen weeks" kinds of things.

All of this was hypothetical though. My maternal instincts were still in hibernation. Fear propelled me forward to the day when I would tell him I was tossing the birth control pills. The press and my doctor had beaten it into me: Everything about a pregnancy is high risk for women over thirty-five, so I knew it was decision time. In December, my tentative campaign started to work. At D's prompting, I ended up in a doctor's office giving blood for HIV, rubella, and hepatitis tests, the holy trinity of pregnancy screening. And then he started harping on about the idea to tell my parents our big plans.

I couldn't really tell him at that point it was all a big bluff, just me hedging my bets in case my hormones starting acting up and I found myself cooing uncontrollably at babies. I had no choice but to go along with his plan, tone it down a bit for sure, but at the end of the day, there wasn't really any excuse not to tell my parents. I was actually finding his desire to please them kind of endearing. Maybe his newfound resolve, plus the unbearable weight of expectation from my parents, would be enough to kick-start my biological clock.

The £400 Fruitcake

A T RODDY'S URGING, our first real social event as part-time residents in the Cotswolds was the Cotswold Hunt Grand Auction. It would be, he said, "a good place to meet the right sort of people." I wanted to ask him why it was necessary for a group of generally wealthy people to raise money at auction for their hobby of chasing foxes around the countryside on horseback, but instead I simply nodded in assent. Prior to this, the sum total of my experience at auctions was the previous summer's village show, where the highest grossing item was a £13 bottle of home-made "vintage" 1996 dry hawthorn wine. We didn't know it yet, but our experience bidding on jams and cakes had left us unprepared for this, an introduction of sorts to Cotswold society.

I studied the Hunt Auction's little green catalog, a supply of which had been left at the wine bar the week before. Reading through the lots was surprisingly entertaining, not to mention a primer to a whole new rural vocabulary of gallops and jollies and such. There were one hundred five of them, and every base was covered. In the realm of the practical, one could bid on a housekeeper for a day, babysitting, house-sitting, an airport chauffeur, or a week's dog boarding in kennels, any of which would be a nice complement to the holiday homes on offer in Provence and Switzerland. Those two hundred fifty grams of Oscietra caviar and the case of Château Beychevelle would also come in handy for a continental outing. Other food on offer included a large game pie, "ideal for your point-to-point picnic"; a side of smoked salmon;

half a lamb, butchered and jointed; a whole, cooked ham joint; a large fruitcake; and an assortment of local pub dinners. You could spoil your horse with equine sports massage, a dentistry session, a few bales of hay, or a portrait. Equestrians could spoil themselves with trail hunting, a jolly on horses, a morning on the gallops followed by breakfast with a trainer, a polo lesson with the mysterious-sounding Lavinia Black, a membership subscription to Cirencester Park Polo Club, shares in a two-horse syndicate, or a dressage lesson. Then there was my favorite: the opportunity to work for half a day with a taxidermist who kindly offered that a "specimen can be provided."

There was also a lot of name-dropping going on in the donor list. Even I, the uninitiated, recognized Captain Mark Phillips (presumably some relation to Zara), Hugh Fearnley-Whittingstall of cooking-TV-show fame, David Hicks (I remembered an India Hicks from the pages of *Vogue* years ago, surely related), and a few local lords.

Lured by the promise of complimentary preview drinks and canapés, we arrived at the village hall in plenty of time. We perused the lots, admiring an old hunting map and arguing over the tastefulness of a pasta bowl decorated with horses, hounds, and a fox. With so many of the lots being experiences rather than loot, the preview was over quickly. We shuffled about the room a bit, generally looked sheepish, then retired to a wall to critique the Toffs, a breed of the English that are found in abundance in the Cotswolds and presumably who Roddy meant when he said "the right sort of people." The closest thing to a Toff in America is an old-money, New England WASP. In England Toffs are "old money" too, only it doesn't matter if their old money is long gone (and in any case, there will probably still be enough for a week in Cornwall in the summer and another in Klosters in the winter). The more defining characteristics are breeding, impeccable manners, a cut-glass accent, and the ability to recognize one another as if Toff was tattooed across his or her forehead.

Corduroy trousers are also a dead giveaway for the male Toff, and Gloucestershire's support of the corduroy industry was on full display that evening. I soon realized that this fabric is the upper-class man's license to dress in loud colors. Never mind if it's electric moss-green, a shade I previously didn't know existed. It's made of corduroy! What made this more remarkable is that the men in attendance were generally the sort who in America would be wearing khakis, a polo shirt in a muted shade, and loafers. But here in the English countryside they wore trousers in rare-steak pinks and sports-car blues, transforming the bottom half of the room into a garish, wide-waled rainbow. One gentleman of about fifty stood out in a mélange of clashing yellows: mustard corduroy trousers paired with a canary-colored checked shirt, and a marigold tie speckled with pheasants. I guessed the trousers had not fit him properly for a good ten years by the way they cupped his buttocks. It looked uncomfortable, but he seemed entirely at ease, a master mingler.

The women fell into two sartorial categories: she-man with wool cape, which D informs me is known as Jolly Hockey Sticks in British vernacular, and horse-chic, which includes rabbit fur vests, tall expensive-looking boots worn over tight jeans, and meticulous haircuts. Both are equally confident and friendly. (I have found there is a refreshing lack of correlation between looks and confidence in England compared to Los Angeles, where confidence is precisely inverse to your weight and directly proportionate to the ratio of designer clothing in your wardrobe.) One of the women in the horse-chic category from the organizing committee approached us and made a bit of friendly small talk, asking us if we'd reviewed the lots.

"Oh, yes, lovely things," I told her.

"Oh, yes," she agreed and confided she was in custody of a number of "at any cost" bids for friends who couldn't make it. The catalog had mentioned Internet bidding at chunt.com (if only I were making that web address up). I should have taken this as another sign this wasn't going to be your average charity auction.

The first lot was dinner for two with a bottle of wine at a pub in the next village. Bidding started at £40, and I went in at £50. In a flash, the gavel came down and I found dinner was mine at £70. Now the auctioneer was asking my name.

"Jennifer," I said.

"Jenni-furr," he repeated back. Was he mocking my American accent?

"Last name?"

I told him, quietly.

"A bit louder please," his matronly sidekick demanded.

This time I nearly shouted, eager for the auctioneer to move on to bidding on a day of trail hunting on the Duke of Beaufort's Hunt so all those Toff eyes would move off me. The flush of early success had been replaced with self-consciousness. D was staring at me in disbelief, as if to distance himself and indicate to everyone in the hall, "my wife may be a stupid idiot who would spend £70 on a pub dinner, but no, not me."

It was not until lot six, "A hunting special large fruit cake" made by someone named Peggy went for £400 after a feverish round of bidding that D conceded that perhaps my £70 pub dinner was not such a bad deal. The bidding continued, and we happily quaffed glasses of red wine while admiring the spectacle.

When the lot consisting of the use of a cherry picker for one week came up, D suggested we bid on it, then park it outside the window of the neighbor who told him that we couldn't park our car on the road outside our cottage. Tipsy, we laughed uproariously at our plan. Shortly into the laugh, I thought, *we are having a spontaneous moment of pure laughter,* and then ruined it by looking around to make sure others in the room, who I hoped may have earlier wondered who are they? were seeing us having our moment of pure spontaneous laughter. This way they would know we, the new people in town, were a fun-loving couple having a smashing time at the auction. I paused then laughed some more to cement the point, which by now had been lost. My attempt to disguise my self-consciousness at being a newcomer had only amplified it.

After the auction ended, we shuffled back for last call at the wine bar, where only Roddy and a gentleman from one village over remained, two more stalwarts in the corduroy rainbow. They compared the total takes of this hunt auction, £34,000, to the auctions of their own hunts, £25,000 and £45,000 respectively, or a decent annual income to most people. During the course of the conversation I also learned that the man from the next village went to Westminster School for Boys, which meant nothing to me until it was explained that it's posh. It was intriguing that someone of this man's age—sixtyish—and accomplishments—a retired banker—was still slipping his school pedigree into casual conversation. I would later learn this habit was a distinguishing mark of the well educated, and that notably the Oxford-educated were compelled to drop this fact into the first sixty seconds of any conversation. When I went to pay for our wine, Roddy informed me that the man from the Westminster School of Boys had taken care of it. My protests were met with an impassive reply of, "No, no, let him pay for it. He's very rich."

Back in London at work on the following Monday, I realized how controversial the hunt is. When I told my coworker, Sally, about our weekend entertainment, she gave me a horrified look.

"You don't support that kind of thing, do you?" she asked, wondering where her fellow yoga-class-attending, public-transport-taking, organic-food-eating colleague had gone.

I reminded her that the nasty part of hunting had been banned for a while now and explained my interest was more Margaret Mead–esque, an observer of the charming local wildlife (by which I mean the Toffs of course, not the foxes). She looked confused but let the matter lie.

Still Sally's reaction had piqued my interest, and when I was back in the Cotswolds the next weekend I decided to conduct a pub survey of country gentlemen and women on the topic of the hunt. Being American gives me a bit of an outsider status that parlays well into nosy, politically charged questions over a glass of wine. I can, if you will, play dumb. And this is how I found out that the most common defense for the hunt is that foxes are vermin. There were many stories of a fox in the henhouse or amongst the flock. There was also the defense of the whole economy built up around the hunt—local caterers and pubs provide breakfast and lunch, not to mention the trade brought in by tourists who come in to watch the whole thing. And there is no denying the social aspect. It is a big all-day party both for the riders and the observers, who move from post to post along the country lanes to get a good view.

Later in February, D and I unwittingly ended up in the midst of a hunt while out on a morning ramble. We first came across a horse-mounted and hunt-attired father and his two sons, around ages eight and twelve, separated from the larger group. We encountered them at a gate and they were disarmingly polite, well-spoken, and self-possessed children as they gave way and let us pass. It was all very "no, you," "no, you," "jolly good," and "tally ho."

People really talk this way in the Cotswolds.

This meeting stirred an epiphany in D. He's from Liverpool, the flag-bearing city for the working man and socialism in the Western world, the kind of place where Michael Moore goes to premiere his movies in the UK. And while they will always have the Beatles, Liverpudlians have a harder time shaking off punch lines about their propensity for stealing and for wearing tracksuits. Although D has transcended his difficult Liverpool upbringing, replete with parental alcoholism and mental illness, the class mythos ingrained in him as a child lives on. He confessed that he half-expected these hunt children to snort with derision while instructing their horses to kick mud on us as they passed. His own class preconceptions, long dormant but still alive, were exposed.

Not long after the hunting-family encounter, the entire hunt party emerged from a deep gully. They charged up a hill, all sharp blue coats and clipped horses, accompanied by a barking pack of hounds. We watched transfixed just a few meters away as the handsome spectacle unfurled itself across the countryside. I wasn't sure we would ever fit in with the Toffs, but we were rather enjoying watching from the sidelines.

Field Guide Number One:

Walk to challenge your social preconceptions

Distance	4 miles (approximately)
Duration	2 hours, plus however long you linger at the pub or watching the hunt
Difficulty	Easy, especially when polite Toff children on horseback open and close gates for you

Rambling, a suitably Brit-eccentric word for what most Americans would simply call walking or hiking, is a sort of religion in rural England. Most landowners give right of way to ramblers, so there's an extensive network of trails across the countryside. I knew I was hooked when I invested a three-figure sum in waterproof apparel in which to undertake this activity, and I thought it only fair that a few of my favorite routes got equal billing alongside hunt auctions and village fêtes. This is the one along which we first saw the hunt. It starts and finishes in Guiting Power, one of the loveliest villages in the Cotswolds and home to the Hollow Bottom, the best place to go to watch horse races on TV. It also passes through the village of Naunton, home to some big-time racehorse farms.

1. Start with tea at the Old Post Office in Guiting Power, now a slightly too tasteful home-goods store/newsstand/café with postal services only once a week. After caffeinating yourself, head left, then right at the bakery, continuing on the lane until you reach St. Michael's Church. Although you haven't yet gone far, it's worth sitting for a while on the bench in the church graveyard to take in the view of the hills.

2. Go back out the church gate you came in, then make a U-turn onto the path signposted WARDEN'S WAY. There's also a green badge on the gate that says GUSTAV HOLST WAY (the composer lived in nearby Cheltenham). Follow it through two more gates, over the field, over the little bridge, and up the path with steps cut into it, then across the next field until you come to the road.

3. Go straight ahead uphill on the road, signposted for Naunton. You will shortly come to a large gate on your left, also signposted WARDEN'S WAY/GUSTAV HOLST WAY. Head right along the path across the open field and then along the ridge of a hill. This is the spot where

we first saw the hunt, but even if none is on offer there should be an assortment of daffodils, rabbits, buttercups, rapeseed, May blossom, blackberries, and pheasants, in rough seasonal order of appearance, to stir your very own epiphanies.

4. Take a left on the road and continue downhill into Naunton. Take the first road on your right and continue until it turns into a path, forking left. You'll soon see the four-sided gables of the fifteenth-century dovecote, which as best as I can tell is a term used to describe a human-sized birdhouse that very rich people built to show how very rich they were in centuries past.

5. Cross the stream and continue up the hill, taking a right at the road. The Black Horse pub is just a few minutes along the road on the left and a worthy-stopping place for lunch, particularly a Sunday roast.

6. Head right out of the Black Horse along the road (briefly retreading your steps), branching right up the hill and past the Baptist chapel on your left. Continue to head right up the steep hill, where, at the top, you are likely to be greeted by racehorses poking their heads out of the narrow windows of a stone barn.

7. Turn left onto the road at the top of the hill, continuing past the horse farm. Take your next left for a short, steep stretch downhill with a view over the grandeur of Guiting Grange. Turn right at the junction, then left opposite the gated main drive to Guiting Grange. This takes you back into Guiting Power along the main lane.

Rural Retail

NOT LONG AFTER the Cotswold Hunt Grand Auction, we made our first real friends in the Cotswolds, Rupert and Ralph. They were weekenders like us, with a beautiful loft flat in a converted Georgian mansion by the church. We met them where we met almost everyone we know in the Cotswolds, at the wine bar, yet I was pretty sure Roddy wouldn't have considered them the "right sort of people." Over several chance meetings and several bottles of Prosecco, I made my way through my list of getting-to-know-you questions. Eventually I worked my way up to the one I was most interested in hearing about: what their experience of being gay was in the Cotswolds, which is, after all, a conservative place. I soon learned Rupert and Ralph read *The Telegraph* and *The Times*. They shoot. They drive a Porsche, a Range Rover, and a Mercedes, the last of which they had just accidentally dinged backing out of the parking lot of their local Conservative MP's (Member of Parliament) house where they had been attending a Pimm's garden party for supporters. (I had forgotten that in England political life is free of the divisive social issues like reproductive and gay rights that dominate American politics, thus freeing up citizens to choose their party allegiance on the basis of actual issues of the state, like fiscal and foreign policies.) On second thought, Roddy probably would have considered them the "right sort of people." The truth is they fit in to Poshtershire way better than D and I ever would, and that's without even factoring my new Toyota Prius into the equation. I was fully prepared for a few cold shoulders at the wine bar once I was spotted around town in an eco-friendly vehicle, perhaps the height of country uncoolness.

D was delighted that we had made the acquaintance of a gay couple. It was nice to have made the acquaintance of any couple, after two years of living in London with hardly any friends outside of work. While D still had London friends from his time living there in his twenties, they were, without exception, now parents of young children. As such, we found our social interactions with them limited to child-friendly activities, of which we soon tired, or the very rare and precious child-free outing, which seemed to occur biannually and be dominated by the parents' desire to get very, very drunk.

But D was particularly delighted to have made the acquaintance of a gay couple because, as Ralph himself would comment a few months after we met, D is gayer than he is. And Ralph was right: D is as lavender as a bluebell is purple. The only notable exception to his lavenderness is that he likes his sex with women. For the most part, this works well in our marriage. He genuinely likes to shop for clothes, is always up for a Hugh Grant romcom, and has handled the interior design in every home we've had. And there was plenty of interior design that had to be done with the cottage.

One of the conditions of closing on the cottage was that the flood damage had to be repaired, which consisted mostly of drying out the first floor with industrial fans and a bit of replastering and painting. We told the former owners not to bother replacing the flooring, which had been a dire duo of wood-effect vinyl in the kitchen and, in the living room, the kind of cheap beige carpeting favored by landlords of student housing. Other unwelcome remnants of the previous owner's taste remained, like the floral polyester curtains in the bedrooms and a marigold velvet curtain that separated the kitchen from the living room. But there was also a woodburning stove and an elm window seat, and for a few weeks if I squinted when I looked at the Egyptian throw rug hiding the concrete floor I could pretend it was almost cozy. But

I had to agree when D finally insisted it was time to make some progress in the cottage-ification of Drovers' interior.

Decorating a rural cottage involved a new retail vocabulary, one that didn't include Habitat—the Pottery Barn of England—or IKEA, both of which had played central roles in decorating our London flat. This was just as well, as I am still emotionally scarred from the evening I spent traversing London's North Circular Road in driving rain to collect the frame of my Hopen wardrobes from one branch of IKEA and the doors from another. Instead decorating in the countryside means flea markets, junk shops that call themselves antiques stores, estate sales, and reclamation yards. It's more scavenger hunt than mall. But before you realize this, you have to get momentarily hypnotized by the Harvey Nichols of the Cotswolds: Daylesford Organic.

At Daylesford, barns have been transformed into a pristine shopping complex in a hamlet not far from the market town of Stow-on-the-Wold. Visitors come from near and far to pay homage to the spiritual home of organically reared, locally produced, seasonal food porn. It makes Chez Panisse look like a shack, a sad imitator, despite being its predecessor. The first building in the complex houses the café cum deli/bakery cum grocery store, and as you approach it, you see an outdoor display of seasonal produce arrayed on stacked antique cartons or a donkey cart or some other suitably rustic stage set. Vegetables are the stars here, and I am sure they have their own stylists. There is also a butcher, stocked by the in-house abattoir, a clothing store, and a spa called The Hay Barn. Our temptation came in the kitchenware and garden shops, filled with distressed yet elegant things in the beiges and pale greens that are so emblematic of Cotswolds exteriors. We admired a birdhouse shaped like a bandstand until I turned over the price tag and saw that it cost £600. This is when I realized that if you were very rich you could furnish your entire Cotswold estate in a single shopping trip to Daylesford, but we would be scouring vintage sales and reclamation yards for years to come.

Still I wanted to buy something at Daylesford, so I settled on a chunk of Parmesan and a zucchini (or a courgette in British English) from the food shop to use for dinner that night. Apparently nobody told the checkout girl, young and stylish in Daylesford's trademark tasteful brown, where she worked.

"This is a courgette, right?" she asked me, holding up the plump green vegetable for examination as if it were a moon rock before plopping it on the scale.

Having come to our senses, we started the redecoration of Drovers in earnest with a visit to the antiques arcade in Cirencester. This Aladdin's cave of fox-hunting prints and horse brasses is far more curated-garage-sale than Christie's, which is just as well given the sticker shock still lingering from Daylesford. We left with a hammered brass coal scuttle and some vintage *Vanity Fair* prints for under £70. I was slightly worried the print depicting a turbaned Punjabi polo player might be construed as racist, but the companion print of a mustachioed, barrel-torsoed Englishman captioned "I Say" looks equally ridiculous. I should have been more worried our cottage was going to look like a pub.

Near the Risdales, we discovered a gigantic reclamation yard, a paradise for newbies like us striving for the Cotswold look. Outside is a vast graveyard for the stone ornaments—toadstools, orbs, troughs, and birdbaths—that are the garden gnomes of the Cotswolds. I had been warned that you can tell weekenders from locals by the reproduction coach lights hanging on their barn conversions. I suspect a disused-wagon wheel in the garden sends the same message, but we got one anyway. (The garden is fenced in, protecting our cliché from public scorn.)

Inside, the proprietor produced a pockmarked length of elm perfect for a mantel piece and a pine ledge-and-brace door for the kitchen (marigold velvet curtain be gone!). D noticed the 1930s suitcase, the one he could decorate with replica vintage luggage labels and plop in that empty spot underneath the stairs, as I was paying for the other stuff. The proprietor threw in the antique ink jars to decorate the chest of drawers and a handful of dusty hardbacks for good measure.

The only foray into a chain retail store was a visit to Laura Ashley, my first since the mideighties when my mother took advantage of the favorable sterling to dollar exchange rate on a summer vacation to festoon my sister and me in yards of floral print, sailor stripes, ruffled blouses, and espadrilles of every color. (An artifact from that vacation that survived, a navy-blue Burberry wax coat, was totally apropos of my new Gloucestershire life. That it is moth-eaten just made it more so). We left Laura Ashley with orders placed for one antiqued brass-effect reading lamp, a saddle-brown leather couch and footstool, and a pair of red and beige gingham-checked curtains to replace the polyester monstrosities. The 1980s floral drop waists with lace collars have long been retired, but our cottage would soon be clad in their interior design equivalent.

Horse Play

And so spring arrived, and with it my packet of six pink foil strips of pills. Between all the house decorating, visits to the wine bar, and auctions, I had hardly had time to think anymore about motherhood. Only when my birth control prescription ran out was I forced to confront my own ambivalence on the matter. And unencumbered by any biological urges, I realized ambivalence was not a foundation that would sustain me, much less my husband, through sleepless nights and chafed nipples. Still I was ill at ease with my choice. I envied those women who have motherhood emblazoned on their brainwaves like Manifest Destiny. I had no tangible reasons to avoid it—good jobs, a home, a willing husband—yet I had no real urge either. More infuriating was that I didn't feel any particular passion about remaining childless. I was on no high horse about what a crappy world it is to bring a child into or that I was saving the planet by not contributing another carbon energy-consuming being to the cosmos. When I held friends' babies in my arms I cooed, enjoyed the baby scent, admired their perfect skin, and marveled at their tiny fingernails. And then, after ten minutes or so, I was happy to hand them back.

D, too, was baffled by this turn of events. But the more I explored this with him the more I realized this had nothing to do with me snuffing out the flame on his burning desire to sire a child. He just wanted me to want to know what I wanted to do, and the fact that I didn't deeply annoyed him. It was a good thing there were more country pursuits teed up to distract us.

In particular, spring in the Cotswolds means horse racing. This is horse country and manicured horse farms dot the hillsides, discernible by jumping equipment that from a distance looks like giant candy-colored matchboxes and pickup sticks strewn about the fields. The racing event of the season is the Cheltenham Festival, for which half of Ireland, also horse mad, descends into Gloucestershire's pubs and inns. Despite my enthusiasm for trying new country pursuits, I didn't manage to book tickets to any of the Cheltenham Festival days. (We had already visited the Cheltenham racecourse for the Sunday flea market, a worthy but entirely different sort of sporting event.) Lots of administrative tasks—paying bills on time, booking train tickets, doing laundry—had gone out the window since buying Drovers Cottage. Chores used to get done on weekends, but now the pressure was on to enjoy ourselves come Saturday, especially if the weather was nice. The manufactured pressure to have a good time, formerly the reserve of real vacations, had with the purchase of a second home become a weekly event. In a fine example of first world problems, we were going to have a good time whether we liked it or not. And in this case, I was too busy having a good time to make time to purchase some tickets that would have allowed us to have, well, a good time.

And so we watched the biggest race of the festival, The Gold Cup, on television. This was a much-publicized battle between elegance in the form of the sleek Kauto Star and brute force embodied in the gigantic Denman. Equally as interesting as the horses was the spectacle of the attendees. The place was swimming in gloriously vulgar hats that are as emblematic of English weddings and horse races as Hermès scarves are of French mademoiselles. I still treasure my own hot-pink, pimp-feathered hat purchased for Royal Ascot the previous year. It may not be as versatile as a Hermès scarf but the opportunities in life to wear vision-obstructing, fuchsia-colored feathers on your head are rare and must be taken. In the end, Denman crushed Kauto Star. It was a victory for brashness of every kind, including big hats.

Our only real horse race of the year took place at the village hall, and there had been much discussion beforehand about what this race would look like since it was being held in a village hall rather than at a racecourse. The consensus between D and Rupert and Ralph, who were going with us, was that it would be betting on prerecorded horse races shown on video monitors. We had gotten a race guide with our prepurchased tickets, each sponsored by local businesses so we could, for example, bet on Lamb Chop to place in the butcher's race.

When we arrived at the hall there were betting booths with visored attendants and a bar set up in the corner. That's where the similarities to a real racecourse ended. Attendees were seated around a giant central checkerboard set out in masking tape. Our assigned table was front and center, so we were on full display to our fellow villagers, like some kind of demented bridal party. Stroppy teenagers, three of each gender, jockeyed rocking-horse-sized wooden steeds painted in bright colors with mop-string hair. (Their parents definitely made them do it.) A tuxedoed MC called for volunteers to throw the giant fuzzy dice, the roll of which would determine the progress of the wooden horses up and back the checkerboard. D, no wallflower, was first to throw.

A childless couple and a gay couple shaken up with a few bottles of wine can be awfully catty. Well, awfully awful really. Between trips to the bar and the betting tables, Rupert and I spent much of our time comparing notes on the relative attractiveness of the teenage jockeys, neither gender spared. In retrospect, this was probably not a good way to endear ourselves to local parents. (We were sure we were whispering, but our perception could have been undermined by our blood-alcohol content.) Ralph then became obsessed with getting a turn at throwing the dice, an activity that had grown in popularity with each passing race. Elbowing small children aside, he finally managed to secure his position as thrower of the dice in the last race, following tense negotiations with the MC on a cigarette break between races five and six.

At the end of the evening, a young man in a wheelchair took
the microphone to thank everyone. He was the beneficiary of the
evening's fundraising, which would go to buy a sports wheelchair he would use to play tennis. He was confident, gracious,
and eloquent, so much so that we immediately sobered up in the
full realization of what a generous community we'd so recklessly
imposed ourselves on. This man didn't need our charity. We were
far more desperate specimens in need of our own fundraiser
to pay for the many hours of psychotherapy we each required.
Through it all our new neighbors sat on either side of us smiling
patiently. We just weren't sure if they would still be speaking to us
in the morning.

The Strange Customs of the English at Play

ON THE FIRST sunny Saturday morning in June, the kettle was boiling and the French press readied when I realized we had no milk. This lack of basic provisions was a familiar annoyance in the weekly back and forth between London and the Cotswolds. With some exasperation, I extricated myself from my pajamas and into clothing marginally suitable for public view. I couldn't be bothered to brush my teeth; I just hoped I wouldn't run into anyone I knew. I soon learned this attitude is a hangover from the urban anonymity of London. You always run into someone you know in the market square.

It's a one-block walk along a stone-wall-lined lane to the shop, along which the village looked like a country-themed It's a Small World ride. Pensioners practically skipped on their way to collect the weekend papers. Four cats frolicked in our lane (cats! in all my years as a cat owner, I'd never seen a cat frolic, yet here they were doing exactly that), while white butterflies skittered above.

Once inside, my shopping list expanded from milk to include two of the freshly baked croissants on offer, a potato and cheese pastie for D, a newspaper, and a basket of raspberries. I decided I needed some of that yogurt made in the next village over to go with the raspberries, so I walked across the green to the butcher who happens to sell it. By now, I was positively buzzing, chatting with the butcher as I juggled my purchases. I couldn't help comparing it to the last time I went to get a pint of milk at the corner store in London: In midflow of taking my money, the shopkeeper spat onto the floor of his own shop. As I walked back to our cottage, I felt an overwhelming urge to quit my corporate London job, take over the village post office, and open a tea shop selling tasteful tchotckes.

Six months in as an official weekend resident, I was still in love with every aspect of village life. In fact, I was most in love with the mundane routines, the pleasure of which seems to have been totally lost in an urban existence. I may have been in love, but I was less sure if the town was in love with us. There was the potential damage we had done on the horse-racing evening, not to mention the fact that we were, after all, still outsiders. And people are suspicious of outsiders in these parts. Residents who've been here for twenty years are careful not to call themselves locals, even if they were born in the village three miles down the road. Even worse we were weekenders, sometimes more sinisterly referred to as incomers, a breed reviled throughout the English countryside. Weekenders drive up property prices so locals can't afford to buy anything, then only use their luxury barn conversions on the occasional long weekend. When they do show up, it's in an enormous, gas-guzzling Range Rover known locally as a Chelsea tractor. I knew all about weekenders because the British media loves to do stories on them. Hardly a month goes by without a sarcastic editorial in our regional magazine, *Cotswold Life,* on these hedge-fund men and their Cath Kidston–print-bedecked wives, children, and kitchens. Channel 4 ran a whole documentary on how weekenders ruined a small Cornish fishing village. To protect against this locust, one member of the Cotswold landed gentry, Lord Vestey, reserves cottages in his hamlet for locals only. According to a tipsy and possibly dubious source at the pub, even the government was out to get the weekender: Second-homers are contributing to the country's housing shortage and legislation or taxation or some equally unpleasant "-tion" was imminent.

You can understand why D and I were worried. We did, after

all, work in London during the week and go to the Cotswolds on, well, weekends. But that's about where the similarities ended. We didn't manage hedge funds or work in any other capacity in "the City." We were devoted to our country cottage and came every weekend without fail. If there was a fête or a church service or a charity event, we'd be there, first in line to buy raffle tickets. And I've never set foot in a Cath Kidston shop in my life.

To prove our worthiness, we embraced the full lineup of fêtes, festivals, shows, plays, operas, and concerts on the Cotswold summer calendar. All of these events are bravely planned for the outdoors, and all were excellent distractions from the question of motherhood. The weather that first summer was marginally better than the summer before, the year of the disastrous Gloucestershire floods, which meant we had about three days of sunshine. We tried our best to make full use of them all. And on this particular morning, the one when the village was looking its rural-themed It's a Small World best, I could think of no better way to make use of the sunshine than by taking a walk.

D, however, was struggling. He was thus far immune to the charms of the outside world, having spent most of the morning whipping himself into a froth triggered by the fact that he left his pants at home in London. This meant he couldn't wear his bermuda shorts on our walk as he intended to do because then he wouldn't have anything to wear out to dinner for the rest of the weekend. This also explained why he was wandering around the cottage stamping his feet and sighing in his best rendition of a seven-year-old girl's temper tantrum.

"I forgot my pants. The weekend is ruined," he announced.

I decided to sit down. This was going to take a while.

After the better part of an hour, D arrived at the simple solution of repurposing his running gear into walking gear. He dressed in an orange, sweat-wicking tank top, black running shorts, hiking boots, mud-protecting gaiters, and a backpack. He looked like a very camp gay pumpkin, but I of course assured him that he looked absolutely fine. At that point, I would have told him he looked fine in a pair of underpants if it would have gotten him to leave the house. As we finally set out on our walk, he was still moaning. Exasperated, I pointed out the skipping pensioners, frolicking cats, and skittering butterflies. He conceded it was an altogether more pleasant sight than the post-Friday-night cider-cans-in-canal tableau we'd face on a morning walk in London.

That D was still kvetching at this point in the day was normal. His path to unwinding on weekends ran like clockwork, starting with clenched muscles and rapid-fire speech as we battled traffic out of London on Thursday or Friday night. This progressed into a near silent, except to complain, tetchiness the next morning before achieving full relaxation sometime that afternoon, usually after a few hours of hard tramping along a ploughed field or at the point on our bike route just after the big hill through Turkdean, when the landscape opens into a wide valley and we're compelled to stop and take it all in. I've tried to tamper with this process in the past to accelerate it, but I've found it's best left to take its course. It's kind of like trying to unwind a really tangled telephone cord. You can mess around with it, looping it through this way and that to untie the knots, but the easiest and most efficient route is just to hold the cord up dangling the receiver, then watch it unwind itself.

I joke about my husband's behavior, but it is all not as light-hearted as the gay pumpkin episode. He had been diagnosed with varying shades of depression over the years and, since moving back to England, had tried medication to treat it. The first prescription that a British doctor gave him was for a medication used to treat incontinence in old ladies that also happens to have some kind of antidepressant side effect. At least that's what the shrink told D, which made both of us wonder about the wisdom of venturing onto the antidepressant meds frontier in the, shall we say, less progressive world of British mental-health care. (Never mind the bedside manner issues associated with telling a depressed, middle-aged, adult male that he's going onto pills that help grannies with wee problems.)

D and I are both veterans of therapy from our years in Los Angeles. In the great nature versus nurture debate, his southern California therapist favored nurture, which in turn led her to an antimedication bias. Her logic was that you need to deal with the underlying issues, not just rely on medication. And so D dutifully dealt with those issues, putting in hard time in both individual and group therapy with me. This gave us both awareness and fluency and comprehension of root causes, all of which were helpful and necessary, but only go so far toward managing the damn thing if you're the person in the thick of it. The problem seems to be that if you are in a very dark place, you can't muster the will to use skills you may have acquired when you weren't in the dark place. You may not even be able to get up off the couch.

The depression kept coming back, as is its habit, until finally it got so bad that D broke with principles and got a prescription. This was not without angst. The abstinence from meds to date had been something of a badge of honor. He was dealing with his demons the hard way, rather like I imagine John Wayne would have done it. There were a few things that helped to rationalize the decision, two of which came from our time as Zen practitioners (also in Los Angeles, go figure). The first was the lesson that, as soon as you recognize you are standing on a position, it's probably worth considering getting off it. The second was the memory of a female priest who practiced with us and was dying of cancer. The pain had become unbearable, but she was wary of going onto painkillers, knowing they would leave her "out of it." The sensei would hear nothing of it, insisting she take the morphine; he called it "dharmacology" to make her feel better about it. And finally, we both realized in a very real, living-up-close-with-the-demons kind of way that, whatever caused what was happening, be it nature or nurture, it was a physiological thing, and it made sense that something that has a physiological effect might help.

The incontinence medicine didn't work out so well. You might not wet your pants anymore, but you'll feel pretty speedy. That's when Ritalin came on the scene, which is better known for treating hyperactive nine-year-old boys than depression. D's inability to focus wasn't of the preadolescent, pogo-sticking around in circles variety. It was more a "what's the point of anything when humans are all shit, yet I still need to get this PowerPoint done by noon" kind of thing. Since it is one of the most life-affecting symptoms of his depression, it's what got treated. And it seemed to work.

This is why it was a surprise when he informed me over the summer that he had decided to take a Ritalin vacation. Specifically, he decided to forego the meds for the three days per week we were in the Cotswolds. He said he felt better there. It was something about the fresh air, the peace and quiet, the wide-open spaces. I bought this, but I also suspected this experiment was borne out of a lingering feeling that the meds were somehow wrong, and now that he had found an escape valve from the stress of London, he thought he didn't or shouldn't really need them.

Earlier in my married life, this news would have caused me great distress. I would have been on the Internet scouring the implications and freaking out that he was making changes to his meds without consulting a physician. But not now. I was married enough to know any protest would be a waste of energy. He was going to do this experiment whether I liked it or not. On the one hand, it's his body, and he has the right to determine what he puts into it. On the other hand, it was asking rather a lot of me. It meant only his work colleagues, some of whom he loathed, would be the beneficiaries of the drugs. Surely as the wife I should have gotten something out of this too. He might have been the lab rat, but I was the hamster's wheel, spinning like crazy, or not, depending on the day's experiment.

The evening following our gay pumpkin walk, we drove over to a grand country-house hotel that was hosting an outdoor opera. Elaborate picnics abounded—crystal flute glasses adorned many a folding table and cravats caressed many a gentleman's throat. We fit in fairly well with our smoked-salmon sandwiches and strawberries, even if our plastic tumblers did expose us as Philistines (not to mention D chasing down photographers from *Cotswold*

Life so he might avail himself for a photo op on the social pages). As night fell, I was most impressed by the appearance of the candelabras. Well, that and the portable bathrooms, the nicest I'd ever seen, all recessed lighting and Molton Brown soap. Thankfully the opera itself wasn't too highbrow. Even without a program, D recognized "the World Cup" song and "the British Airways ad from the eighties" song.

Sunday afternoon, we headed off with our neighbors—who had politely declined to mention anything about the evening at the races—to a hog roast and jazz concert in the field behind the village hall in Guiting Power. Without aid of a portable marquee (the hallmark of the truly seasoned British picnicker), we roasted to the tunes of Artie Shaw. By the second bottle of cava, we resorted to putting up rain umbrellas for shade. Our collective stamina was as resolutely British as it had been several weeks earlier when we sat through three rain-soaked hours of outdoor Shakespeare under blankets and brollies. This was our summer and, damn it, we were going to have it.

In July and August, the acid yellow of rapeseed gave way to chunky, sage-green foliage, threaded through with papery poppies in a lurid shade of coral usually favored by little old ladies for lipstick. Green seas of wheat faded into bleached wisps standing on end like a blond shot through with static electricity. Only plumes of cow parsley persisted, party favors of spring. During these months, we worked our way through village fêtes like greedy children with a box of chocolates. I learned firsthand the strange customs of the English at play, which included a rudimentary form of bowling called Skittles, a rubber boot–throwing contest called wang the wellie, and the mysterious-sounding coconut shy. The last consisted of hurling balls at coconuts perched on stakes like shrunken heads. There was always a dog show with more ribbons on offer than dogs in the village, my favorite of which was for the dog with the waggiest tail. Don't forget the Tombola, which, as far as I can tell, is a raffle of the most mundane items the ladies of the village could find lingering in their pantries. (I won a bottle of storebought lemon curd that was nearing its sell-by date.) Of course, there are tea and cakes on hand to sustain you throughout.

The traditional end to the summer festival season is the Last Night of the Proms. Every year the BBC stages this multiweek classical music festival at the Royal Albert Hall in London. My employer owned a box there, and, in years past, I had succeeded in nabbing tickets to a few nights. But this year, the private-equity firm that now owned the company was either filled with classical music nuts or the box had been disposed of in the latest wave of cost cutting. Either way, no Proms tickets were forthcoming.

Luckily, I noticed a sign for a Last Night of the Proms charity event on a bicycle ride around the Cotswolds. We packed a picnic and headed off to the cricket pitch in Naunton on an early August evening, one of the few dry and mild ones of summer. Like our evening of outdoor opera earlier in the summer, British picnicking prowess was on full display. I watched as one trio in front of us planted two stakes in the ground then laid a third across the top, half expecting them to next produce a whole pig for roasting from their wicker basket. Instead they used their spit to hang a colorful array of paper lanterns, which later illuminated important activities like wine pouring. D spotted his doctor sitting in front of us—not the one who had prescribed the wee medicine for grannies, but a local general practitioner he had acquired since our arrival in the Cotswolds to deal with his more mundane yet routine bouts of hypochondria. This sighting stopped him from rolling a cigarette until the end of the evening, while I coveted the doctor's serious picnic utility chairs—chrome with handy side tables attached—on which he and his family balanced healthful plates of poached salmon and rice salad. We were only slightly self-conscious that our dinner was composed entirely of cheese and wine.

The London Gala Chamber Orchestra started the evening off with an overture to *Orpheus in the Underworld,* which somehow morphed into the can-can. My musical education continued as I learned "O, Danny Boy" is really called "Derry Air." The evening progressed in this vein of songs familiar enough for clapping or singing along, both heartily encouraged by the conductor. Such "let yourself loose" occasions are rare for the tone deaf like me, and I belted out "I Could Have Danced All Night" with abandon.

The crowd had worked itself into a champagne frenzy for the firework finale set to "Jerusalem" and "Land of Hope and Glory," complete with flag waving. This was mostly of the £1 plastic Union Jack variety, but a group that had clearly done this before was equipped with large Scottish, English, and South African flags. I've heard people dismiss this behavior as jingoistic in the past (flag waving and "Jerusalem" are also a traditional part of the real last night at The Proms), but from my foreigner's point of view, it all seemed harmless enough. The only sinister hint was when an overly enthusiastic middle-aged gent rushed the stage during "Rule, Britannia!" to stare into the soprano's eyes at uncomfortably close range. If I'd had an American flag, I would have joined in and had the Fourth of July experience I'd been deprived of the previous month.

The evening ended with a reprisal of the can-can, during which the audience was invited down front. One pink-chinoed Toff found himself flat on his back in his haste to descend the hillside. The potent combination of champagne consumption and embarrassment had him back on his feet in plenty of time to high-kick his heart out. I hoped for my husband that the combination of Ritalin and fresh air would someday soon make him feel cheery enough to high-kick his heart out too.

Field Guide Number Two:

Walk for when you've forgotten your pants, a.k.a. the gay pumpkin walk

Distance	11 miles (approximately)
Duration	4 hours, plus however long you linger at the pub or stop to admire the view from Yanworth
Difficulty	Moderate

Despite taking a long time to get started on our first attempt at this walk, it has since become a favorite. (It also helps that D's closet is now well stocked with both walking shorts and trousers at the cottage.) It starts and finishes in the market town of Northleach, looping through Yanworth, skirting the Chedworth Roman Villa, pausing at the Fossebridge Inn, and passing back through Coln St. Dennis.

1. Head out of Northleach on All Alone. Take care crossing the busy A429 and continue up the lane. At the first crossroads, go straight and stay on the right side of the road, where you will immediately see a small stone stile.

2. Head right across the field and follow it around for about ten minutes until you see a gate. Go through the gate and continue straight on, mingling with sheep as you go, until you reach Oxpens Farm. Go left and cut through the farmyard, joining the dirt track heading uphill into the hamlet of Yanworth. There is a bench outside the chocolate-box church, but the best views are farther up the road where residents are treated to sweeping views of their landlord's, Lord Vestey's, Stowell Park estate. (Once or twice a year, the gardens of Stowell are open to the public, complete with tea and cakes served in the ballroom.)

3. Continue on the road, turning right at the sign for the Roman Villa. If you're a fan of Roman history or gladiator demonstrations by middle-aged men of questionable fitness, then it's worth stopping for a while at this National Trust site. If not, take the left onto the dirt road before the hill up to the Villa.

4. Follow the road around as it skirts the lovely River Coln until you meet the paved road again. Head straight down, following the signs for Fossebridge. There's a gravel

driveway at the back of the grounds of the Fossebridge
Inn. Take that and enter the pub from the back door.
(If you come to the busy A429, you've missed the back
entrance, but the inn is just to your left.)

5. Leave the pub through the front, taking care as you cross
   the dip in the busy A429. There is a stile directly across
   from the pub that leads you into a field, then up to the
   road in Coln St. Dennis. Turn left and follow the signs
   for Northleach, staying on the road for the last couple of
   miles.

New Town

SWINDON IS A "NEW TOWN," which is British for a town that architects forgot. Over the summer, I went for an interview there for a job as an IT director at a computing society. I did not want to be the IT director at a computing society—a job no kid dreams of growing up to do—but my company was in the middle of laying off half its global workforce, so it seemed like I should at least take advantage of the interview practice.

D was excited about this interview. He would have been excited if I had an interview for a job as a window washer in Swindon. This is because Swindon is within commuting distance of our cottage in the Cotswolds, and he had started to crave a full-time life there. This job in Swindon brought him one step closer to that reality: I could live full-time in the Cotswolds, we could sell or rent our London flat, and he could downsize to a studio during the week when he needed to be there. He thought if I jumped first onto the full-time rural-life wagon, it would embolden him to eventually do the same. I thought he was a chicken.

We decided to drive to Swindon on the Sunday before the interview to scope it out. It was raining and cold, and there was supposedly a movie theater there to help us take our minds off the fact that, meteorologically speaking, we didn't seem to be having a summer. We drove to the train station first. D loves train stations and bemoaning the demise of the steam railways that used to connect many of the villages in the Cotswolds. Aesthetically the Swindon railway station was somewhere between a mental institution and a jail and, needless to say, devoid of any of the romance associated with trains. To make matters worse, Swindon in the rain was the most depressing place I've ever been, a slick of seventies concrete accented in dung brown. How could a city on the edge of the Cotswolds, a designated Area of Outstanding Natural Beauty, look this way? It shouldn't be allowed. I was impatient and wanted to leave the train station. D shouted, I pouted, and we drove back to our cottage without seeing a movie.

After the interview, I was slightly more optimistic about Swindon. The building was in an office park with all the charm of Heathrow, but you got your own parking space. With three years of London buses and tubes under my belt, the idea of driving to work and having a parking space reminded me of life in Los Angeles in a good way. The man who interviewed me and would be my boss was nice; he was someone I could work for, which I've learned the hard way is no small thing. As he walked me out of the office after the interview, he pointed out a basket of fruit on a filing cabinet and informed me that free fruit was a perk of working at the company. He was being serious. I didn't think it a good time to tell him we had a subsidized bar and restaurant at my current office.

On some level, I knew it was unrealistic to think I could work in a building that looks like the inside of the Mondrian Hotel on the Sunset Strip forever, especially now that the record company where I worked was owned by a cost-conscious private-equity firm. But for now, that was where I worked, all gleaming white and glass, nestled in the posh London neighborhood of Kensington, moments away from Hyde Park and Holland Park and the only Whole Foods in England.

As it turned out, I would be staying in close proximity to absurdly priced produce for a little while longer. I didn't get the job in Swindon. Never mind how I felt about the town or the company's humble idea of employee perks, my pride was hurt. Within a few weeks, the edge was taken off when I learned I managed to keep my London job despite the latest round of layoffs. Still the idea of a full-time life in the Cotswolds had taken root.

In fact, it only took three more months until the proverbial organically reared carrot was dangling in front of me in the form of a job offer that was a commutable distance from our Cotswold town, blessedly not in Swindon. All my big talk about life in the country was being put to the test, and so I did what I do with any big decision. I made a list. It looked something like this:

Pros:

1. I got a job offer in the midst of one of the largest global economic meltdowns in history. When I got the call, I was standing in the lobby of a gothic building in London watching BBC News announce the bottom had fallen out while lots of besuited bankers looked on in horror. In other words, don't look a gift horse in the mouth.

2. I could live in the Cotswolds full-time.

3. The music industry, provider of my current job, is dying and still has no credible strategy for survival. Potential new company has strategy. They even talked about it during my interviews. Hurrah! How novel.

4. New boss-to-be seems like the kind of guy I could get along with.

Cons:

1. D and I would live apart two nights per week. Or is this a pro? Still trying to work this one out. He is so obsessed with work right now that most nights in London are spent zoned out in front of the TV when he finally does arrive home sometime after 8:00 PM. Is this any different than being apart?

2. Gas costs. Would have to drive to new job. Something about a petrol card in contract that I must investigate, not to mention must get British driver's license!

3. One-hundred-ten-mile round-trip commute. Have never had a serious commute, even when I lived in Los Angeles. Am trying to think about bright side. Could download KCRW podcasts for the ride and pretend like I am now a Southern California commuter.

4. Cotswold house is a postage stamp intended for weekending. Then again London flat is a postage stamp. Need somewhere to hang all my clothes in the Cotswolds. Damn England and its lack of built-in closets.

It was four–all.

The Mistress

SINCE WE STARTED weekending in the Cotswolds, D and I had gotten in the habit of going to church a couple of Sundays a month, something neither of us had done since childhood when our mothers dragged us along to Church of England and Presbyterian services, respectively. My mother used to bribe my sister and me with a breakfast of cherry cake and lemon-filleds from the Mister Donut drive-thru on the way there. In my early teens, I was more motivated because attending church youth group guaranteed your spot on the annual Sugar Mountain, North Carolina, ski trip and because there were boys. Then I went through an odd couple of evangelicalish years in high school, courtesy of a school club called Fellowship of Christian Athletes. My mother and lapsed-Catholic father didn't seem to notice my newfound interest in the Bible and generally being a judgmental prat. I guess when you're the parents of a teenager, you can imagine worse things and choose your battles.

And then there was a religious dry spell until D and I started attending a Zen center in Los Angeles, one of those things, like therapy, that seems more plausible in Los Angeles and was not a habit that stuck with us in London. I'm not sure how to explain the return to the fold, except that an hour's contemplation seems congruous with the countryside in a way it never did in London, despite the rigors of a Church of England matins. It has something to do with the natural beauty of the setting and the history and architectural interest of the churches themselves. Most of all, it had to do with the congregation, which, excluding us, numbered six elderly ladies. We had grown fond of them, especially the feisty, ninety-year-old Dorothy, who owned the local bakery and still added up purchases by hand to keep her mind sharp. She always seemed so pleased to see us, and neither of us wanted to disappoint.

Most Sundays, a good sing-song in church was enough to power D through the day. But on this particular autumn weekend, the hymns weren't enough to hold back his plunge into depression. I had almost forgotten about it over the past few months, buried as it was underneath a patch of work-related mania. Of course I knew the early mornings and late nights and the fact that the only conversations that seemed to hold his attention were job-related was unhealthy. Work was just the latest version of a lid on the boiling pot of his depression, even if, as far as coping mechanisms go, it was preferable to watching him spend four-hour stretches on the couch watching repeats of daytime-television property shows, which had been the defining characteristic of his last bout with the demon disease.

This is how the dynamic of depression works in our relationship. There's a good patch of days or weeks or even months, fuelled by meds or work success or some other stroke of luck. Things are so normal that when a depression does set in—and it always does—I feel shocked. It's as if an old lover of his has shown up at the door and asked, straight-faced, to come in for a shag with him. How dare she come back after all this time? Yet I know I have to let her in, and she'll stay as long as she likes. My efforts to expel her with logic and reason and breaking-down problems into manageable chunks just leave us both feeling exasperated. All the while, the mistress waits patiently on the couch for me to exhaust myself and stomp out of the room.

This time, the mistress brought along the same old baggage, conflating every issue related to my new job offer with D's lifetime history of regret and resentment. Gone was his encouragement and infectious enthusiasm that prompted me to look for a job in the countryside in the first place. Instead there was a whole raft of unattractive insecurities that, in their essence, amounted to a concern over who was going to take care of him if I was spending all my time in the Cotswolds. Next time, perhaps the mistress could be polite enough not to show up in the middle of a life-changing decision, although she's never been known for her tact.

By the time I walked into the wine bar that night, I was primed for some words of wisdom, some advice, a sign from God—anything really that would help me decide whether or not to take this job. It was a slow night and Roddy, perhaps bored, obliged.

"When life opens a door, you have to go through it," he responded upon hearing my dilemma.

That was it. A perfect, if clichéd, summary of what I had to do. This job was on the table and I had to take it.

But wait, what was Roddy talking about now? Something about that miserable time when he ended up in a job he wasn't suited for through the happenstance of being in the right place at the right time. Had Roddy also been wondering why I had been made a generous offer to do a job I had never really done before after only one in-person meeting?

Useless old Roddy. Useless old husband. I was on my own with this decision.

The Cotswold Cult

I WAS CERTAIN D had been invited to join a cult. It happened, as these things do, in the wine bar. It was empty and lacking promise when we arrived. Harold, de facto town elder and wine-bar fixture, was sitting alone at the head of the big wooden table. He was dressed, as always, in a coat and tie and nursing his habitual glass of red wine. D sat down next to him.

This would not have been my first choice. Despite the fact that I've been introduced to Harold about ten times, he never seems to recognize me when I greet him. Instead he always asks me the same question—"Canadian or American?"—before proceeding to list off his favorite places in America (Burlington, Vermont and Seattle, Washington), then the other places he has visited in America (San Francisco and Minneapolis). He also hogs the communal potato chips, secure in the knowledge that most people consider it rude to try to capture back a bowl of potato chips from a senior citizen. I, however, am not most people.

I would have been happy with an interaction with Harold that consisted solely of some eye contact and a smile on my way to a stool at the bar. But no, here I was sitting at the big wooden table helping him remember the name of Burlington. It's all D's fault. He has a soft spot for old people, honed by a mother who was old before her time.

Harold was in a talking mood, and once we got past the litany of American cities, I learned more about him. He's eighty. He was born in London—Holborn, to be exact. He moved to our

Cotswold town when he was an infant, and, although he has traveled the world, he has always called this place home. At least that's what I think he said.

I have trouble understanding Harold. It's not a volume thing. I just lose track of the words somewhere between his gruff tone and the British accent. He also punctuates every few sentences with a sharp "ha!" which serves many different purposes including "harrumph," "doh," a check to see if you are paying attention, and an exclamation as if to say "isn't that the most marvelous thing ever!"

To get by in a situation like this, I play a game where I infer what he says based on the words I think I understand. There are enough cues to know when to nod or smile or look suitably outraged. It's like when I learned Italian, nodding vigorously upon detecting the words birra or gelato. And, like learning Italian, it gets easier the more you drink.

I'm foggy on details, but other ground covered in the evening with Harold included his stint in the Palestinian police, which had previously been corroborated by other wine-bar sources who added the further embellishment of "a personal friend of Arafat's"; coming face-to-face with a herd of water buffalo in Canton; a Polish girlfriend killed in America in 1951; a Canadian girlfriend; a Romanian girlfriend; Stevie Winwood, a Cotswold resident and wine-bar standard name-drop; a famous-boxer-turned-Honolulu-hotel-bar-piano-player; and the leap, an exclusive, black-tie, annual village event that involves lots of speeches and drinking.

It was the last one that got my attention, in part because Harold had made a point to say no women were allowed. There was also a moment of awkwardness when Harold asked another gentleman at the table, a longtime resident, if he had ever attended. He had not, so Harold chose that moment to ask D—and only D—to write down his name and address, which he said he would give to his secretary to get him on the invite list. The elderly do passive-aggressive very well.

Our good-byes included an admonition to D to reply swiftly

when the invite arrived. My curiosity was piqued, and my money was on the Freemasons.

A few weeks later I was wedged underneath a London conference-room table struggling to unplug my laptop, when a man popped his head in to ask if the room was free. With my rear end still in the air, I answered yes. As I got up to leave, it was apparent that this man thought he knew me. He inquired if by chance I had been in a butcher shop in our Cotswold town over the weekend wearing cycling clothes. I replied that I had, while wondering what the chances were of being caught in two compromising situations in one week by the same person.

It turns out I was not the only employee of my company to have discovered the charms of our lovely little Cotswold town. This man had lived there for sixteen years, enduring the commute into London every day. We exchanged lots of twee gushing about our town, like the joy of walking out your front door to pick blackberries for a cobbler. Then he started telling me about an annual town dinner called the Leet, and it clicked that this was what Harold was describing to us at the wine bar a few weeks prior. My vision of a Cotswold cult was wide of the mark, but this is a case where truth is better than fiction. It's the kind of thing that an American eats up about living in England, almost as much as having a house with a name. Even D was charmed by the revelation.

The Court Leet dates back to 1227 when King Henry III granted our town a charter entitling it to a weekly market. The townsmen have an unbroken record of meeting for the Leet every year since to elect honorary officials to oversee the market. Their duties include making the rounds of the local pubs and reporting on the quality of the brews. The Leet is a sort of State of the Union, only about important things like beer. Children get in on the action too, roaming the streets banging tin cans. When they knock at your door, you are supposed to ask them who the new high bailiff is and give them a coin for their can, a capitalist version of Halloween.

An invitation is a tricky thing, fraught with sensitivities. Some men who have been resident for years have yet to receive one, like the man at the table at the wine bar. If Harold pulled it off for D, it would be a coup. I wasn't banking on it as Harold is prone to bluster, but for D's sake I hoped it would come through.

After some cajoling, Harold did produce the promised ticket to the Court Leet for D. It was held on a Thursday night at the village hall and, being female, I was banished to dinner at the inn across the street with several wives/partners of the attendees, at least one of whom considered the proceedings next door sexist. I, on the other hand, had been married long enough to be grateful for a little time off. I suspect other wives feeling just like I do have played a vital role in keeping this tradition going for the last seven-hundred-odd years.

When the menfolk arrived at the inn just after midnight, they were weary from the speeches, which by all accounts were a bit average that year in everything except duration. I was pleased to hear our neighbor had been elected the new high bailiff. I like him because he is nice and often wears a coral-colored Benetton sweatshirt with a cravat, and without irony. Others are less readily charmed by a cravat. One source, who shall remain unnamed, went as far as to inform me that the new high bailiff is the most boring man in town, which didn't bode well for the next year's speeches.

As it would turn out, D wouldn't have to sit through the following year's speeches because he wouldn't be invited back. In his rushed attempt to make it from London to the Court Leet on time, he had not changed out of the jeans he had worn to work. After the event, we would find out that this sartorial faux pas had caused great offense amongst the High Council of Elders, D's term for the self-appointed important men of the town, who thankfully did not include Roddy. All of a sudden, the advice our neighbor had given us that it was best to stay out of village politics made perfect sense. (I had learned this firsthand earlier in the year when my offer to plant geraniums in the market square—part of the town's efforts in the Britain in Bloom competition—had been rebuffed because the person in charge of the flower committee had not approved of my "rowdy behavior" at local weekend cricket matches.) Now we just had to find a way to entertain ourselves through the upcoming cold months without causing any further scandal.

Autumn

I N NOVEMBER, the cold set in, taking root in our stone house. The electric heaters—there is no gas in our town—in each room seem to be positioned more for aesthetics than utility. All are next to doors or windows so most of the expensive heat they do produce is instantly leeched away. The only real way to heat the house is to light the woodburning stove. When it gets going, the flames beat against the glass door, making a sound loud enough that I once got out of bed to investigate, thinking there was some kind of commotion going on in the narrow pedestrian lane behind our cottage where the local teenagers like to loiter. I soon grew accustomed to the pleasant cacophony of the flames and the clicking refrigerator, the latter of which must be a war wound from its tenure in the floods.

The absence of noise in the countryside amplifies what sound there is. There's the predictable birds and church bells, but also the whistle of wind blowing through hollow-metal gateposts on an afternoon walk, a sort of homemade woodwind, and the booming noises on our morning run, bass-heavy gunshots or explosions from a quarry.

On one of these cold November nights, I ran into Jonny the local shepherd at the wine bar. (I love being able to say I know a real-life shepherd.) Jonny is rather hunky and the object of admiration by both D and Abigail, the lecherous older woman of the town. Abigail is sixtyish, extremely Toff, and divorced because, in her own words, she no longer has any use for a husband. She has the ramrod posture of the horsewoman she is and is generally well-put-together, except for that time when, in the inimitable Toff I-don't-give-a-shit way, she appeared at the wine bar without her dentures. When she speaks to Jonny, she stares at the chest hair protruding from the top of his shirt, in much the same way that I imagine men address her not-inconsiderable bosom.

D admires Jonny because he is a man who lives off the land, someone who toils with his hands. My husband has had a lot of jobs, but never any that required much in the way of physical labor, and he imbues this facet of Jonny with a sort of mystical quality. Jonny is also quick-witted—a prerequisite for respect from D—and extraordinarily at ease with himself for a man of twentysomething. There is a certain wisdom about him that implies age but without any of the associated world-weariness. If our cottage is the architectural manifestation of an ideal of simplicity, Jonny is the living, breathing incarnation of it, or at least he is in D's mind.

I patiently waited my turn with Jonny while Abigail and D fawned, then, at an opportune lull, struck up a conversation about sheep farming. Thinking of my own arctic house, I asked him if sheep are brought inside at night in this cold weather. The answer is no, but in the process of telling me this, he also explained the origin of the word Cotswold, which I was surprised I didn't know after almost a year of being here. *Wold* means "rolling hills" and *cot* refers to an old stone sheep shelter. It literally means a place to sleep in the hills, which reminded me of one of the reasons we were motivated to buy a cottage here in the first place: to escape from the noise of London and get a good night's rest.

This is not the first time I've learned something new in the wine bar. I learned pretty much everything I need to know about life in the country from its patrons. Well, at least everything I need to know to sound marginally credible when talking about life in the country to someone in a pub. And the sum total of Things I Learned in Country Pubs is:

How to play Shove Ha'penny, a Victorian pastime played with the aid of a small blackboard, which is rather dull unless you turn it into a drinking game

The difference between straw and hay; a stag and a buck; a meet and a meeting

What a gilet is—a quilted nylon vest that's de rigueur country attire—and how you pronounce it

How to make a dry martini

How to make an extra-dry martini

The hierarchy of gamekeeping: gamekeeper, beat-keeper, and underkeeper

What a muntjac is and that they taste good

The perfection of a pickled egg nestled in a bed of potato chips

A gun dog bringing back four partridges at once is a bad thing

When snipe season starts

How to make damson gin (said to be good for cold days on the links) and that I enjoy fruited gins of most varieties

Why Chinese takeout restaurants in the UK serve french fries (I'll explain this later, but for now your hint is Butlins.)

How to herd sheep on a steep hill

A joke about a Yorkshire butcher

An inn to visit in the Forest of Bowland

The instructions for the dry martini and the extra-dry martini were provided by the late, legendary David Foster-Ward and require going to New York in the nineteen seventies and grabbing a stool at the old Oak Bar at the Plaza Hotel. Upon ordering a dry martini from Bill the bartender, he would simply hold up the glass of vodka and whisper the word "vermouth" over it. If you ordered an extra-dry martini, Bill would call the bartender at the Waldorf Astoria and have him say "vermouth" over the phone as he held the glass up to the receiver.

The autumnal social calendar included a bingo fund-raiser for the cricket club in the village hall, which left me very disappointed with the British. Instead of yelling "bingo!" when they got a line, they simply raised an arm, signaling the monitor to come check their card. I vowed to D to uphold the American bingo tradition of oral exuberance should my numbers come in. But when, in game six, they did, so did self-consciousness and up went my right arm. Despite my cultural betrayal, I was rewarded with a bottle of Croft Original Pale Cream Sherry, the label of which D decorated with pink polka dots using his bingo dabber pen. I was making up for an adult lifetime of shattered California Lotto dreams with the excellent odds of village life. The weekend before, D won a bottle of champagne in the raffle at a wine-tasting fundraiser for the local school. Between this and the sherry, we were practically stocked for Christmas.

This time of year, the Cotswold palette is still predominantly green, but the big bingo dabber in the sky has added great orbs of lemon-rust and green-gold. Leaves are falling and the autumn colors have peaked. The scenery changes less dramatically week by week than it does in the spring and summer, but it will still be a surprise to show up one weekend soon to find the desolation of bare branches and darkness, especially now that the clocks have turned back. Just before dusk, rays of sunlight broke through the canopy of gray turning the blobs of fall color into glimmering, quaking masses. It looked just like a picture D bought earlier in the year, a watercolor scene of a lone huntsman, and his first foray into art collecting.

I suspect that purchase from a local gallery was as motivated by a desire to be accepted within his new community as it was by the object itself. The gallery owner was Miles, our resident raconteur, occasional bartender at the wine bar, writer, painter, and father of Jonny the shepherd. D and I had enjoyed a bit of banter with him at the wine bar, but it was mostly done from the sidelines. This purchase had finally broken the ice on the friendship, but I was still condescending about D's taste in art. To start with, the painting is stereotypical: huntsman and his horse, a fox, and a dry stone wall. Then there was the fact that, other than scratching their noses and feeding them apples, D and I are about as far away from horse people as you can get. Buying this picture struck me at best as disingenuous, at worst embarrassingly obvious—like something Tony Soprano might pick if he uprooted his family from New Jersey to the Cotswolds.

D prevailed in the face of my self-consciousness. Not only did he buy the hunt scene, a few weeks later he bought a Cecil Aldin etching, the exterior of a rural pub framed on the left by a gnarled old oak, at another local gallery. At this rate of spending, I no longer needed to feel sheepish about the amount of free wine we were quaffing at these monthly show openings. And the huntsman, now standing watch over our bed, has grown on me over time too. I considered transplanting the Gilbert and George print from our London flat for this spot but thought better of it. Irony just doesn't go with ticking stripe and gingham.

Remembrance Day came later in the month. Our local service started with the blessing of a new standard for the village Brownie troop, done with an abundance of pomp and circumstance by Godfrey the vicar, who has a name made for the job. After church, the entire congregation, swollen to twenty or so for the special occasion, filed down the lane to the war memorial on the green for the act of remembrance. Around the British Isles, many others gathered at village greens just like this to speak the names of the war dead and observe two minutes of silence.

A retired local serviceman read aloud the names of those

who died from this village and its sister village up the road, then placed a wreath of poppies on the memorial, followed by another from the Brownies. There were no more than twenty or so war dead, but these are tiny villages and the sense of loss must have been overwhelming. Ninety years later, there were still tears. "The Last Post," the British version of "Taps," played from a portable CD player propped on a chair outside the house at the top of the green. Even the white terrier accompanying his master looked solemn and sat quietly on his haunches throughout.

Afterward we went for a walk, where, despite being intermittently pelted with freezing rain, we were offered two signs of hope and renewal. First was Hawling Lodge, which we watched emerge from ruin over the last year. It has been beautifully restored, including a length of dry stone wall where new, honeyed pieces sit alongside sections dark and chalky with age. A hill serves as one border in the back garden, and there is a door built into it that I would dearly like to open to discover what secret grotto lies within. Later, walking back by Roel Farm, a double rainbow appeared: two perfect arches over ochre fields. Unfortunately there was another reminder on that afternoon in Hawling, a reminder of something I had been trying hard to forget.

Gluttony in Gloucestershire

WHILE MUCH OF MY RURAL EDUCATION is supplied by the patrons of the wine bar, some comes via television. This is how I learned, courtesy of an episode of Hugh Fearnley-Whittingstall's *River Cottage*, that the colored markings on a sheep's behind indicate whether or not she's been shagged. A device harnessed to the ram's chest supplies the dye.

On our recent walk near Hawling, a ewe had looked me straight in the eye, then began stamping her front hooves like a demanding child. She had a freckled face and excellent posture. She stamped some more before turning away to reveal that her entire back half was covered in orange. Apparently the ram in this field liked sassy types. A second look around proved the ram in this field wasn't picky. The pasture was a walk of shame on a grand scale, a virtual promenade of harlots with orange bottoms everywhere. I felt a bit sorry for those few gals that hadn't seen any action, their still-white coats a prudish badge. And I felt some empathy: Eleven months after I'd first said I would try, I still had no desire to get knocked up either.

Mr. Fearnley-Whittingstall also provided an explanation for the sudden appearance of all these orange backsides: If you want a lamb for Easter, the rams need to make a visit by Guy Fawkes, the fifth of November. The technical term for the mating season is the *rut,* a word which has several definitions including "a recurrent period of sexual excitement in certain male ruminants" and "a fixed, usually boring routine." I guess it depends if you ask the ram or the ewe. What was clear to me was that I was in a rut of my own when it came to the subject of motherhood. And what with our impending holiday visit to my parents, I was going to have to come up with some answers soon.

My education in how food makes it to the table didn't stop with Mr. Fearnley-Whittingstall. One Friday night at the wine bar, Georgina the barmaid asked D if he shoots. The sum total of his firearms experience is one morning downing clay pigeons on a north Yorkshire estate. I can better this, having once been taken by my father to a shooting range where we practiced with a pyramid of A&W Root Beer cans in a swampy Florida field. After a moment's pause to consider if any of this qualified, he answered no.

Georgina doesn't shoot either. She was asking because she just bought a bird plucker and was trying to drum up business amongst the local sport shooters. She went on to describe how her new piece of culinary apparatus works like an Epilady for poultry.

I admire Georgina for her entrepreneurial streak. She had recently split from her partner, whom it has been indicated to me in hushed tones was someone of note in the horsey set, but seemed to have wasted no time getting on with it. In addition to her wine bar duties, she had launched a home-cooked meal service that had already supplied us with a Thai red curry for a dinner party. Now the mechanical duck plucker. She was the embodiment of the plucky (no pun intended), pull-yourself-up-by-the-bootstraps, country-gal archetype. I never got to know her well, but in the short time that I did she represented to me a bit of what Jonny represented to D: an idea, admittedly part fantasy, of what a simple life in the country could be. In my eagerness to root for her and all she represented, I wanted to take up shooting just so I could give her bird Epilady some business.

The turkey for our Thanksgiving feast was locally sourced,

although as far as I know, Georgina's Epilady had no role in denuding it. It took some coaxing by the local butcher to secure it since most British poultry farmers prefer to fatten up their turkeys for Christmas, when they can get more money for them. I cooked for D and the neighbors, and the evening went off without a hitch, other than the disappearance of twenty gourmet marshmallows that dissolved into my sweet potato casserole because I left it in the oven too long. (It took visits and inquiries to no fewer than five London shops, including Selfridges, to find those marshmallows. When a specialist American candy shop in Covent Garden couldn't help, I conceded to the artisan fluff on offer at Whole Foods at a cost of approximately thirty-five pence per marshmallow, only to find a jumbo bag of the things at a gas station about two miles from our cottage in the Cotswolds.)

There were some minor concessions to this being a British Thanksgiving, including substituting brussels sprouts and roasted potatoes for peas and mashed potatoes, adding a cheese course, and the fact that there were pheasants alongside the turkeys on my printed novelty napkins. I enjoyed being the cultural authority for the evening—there are not many occasions for this as an American in Britain—and made everyone go around the table and say what they were thankful for.

The indulgent descent toward Christmas continued the following Friday with the Fat Boys lunch, an event D had been invited to by Miles, and for which I had been enlisted as a driver. D was titillated by his inclusion and spent the morning weighing his clothing options aloud like a teenage girl anguishing over her prom dress. Coral-colored cashmere sweater vest or tweed blazer? Was his sheepskin coat "too urban"?

The arrangement was to meet at the wine bar at noon. At 12:30 PM D was just wrapping up a work call, so I was dispatched to the wine bar on my own to stall for him. I used the time to inquire about the etymology of the lunch's name since the attendees, while not in danger of anorexia, were neither overtly fat nor boys. Miles attempted to explain as he poured me half a glass of champagne. The account was delivered in an authoritative and confident voice that tricked me into believing it was a coherent response, a common characteristic of the posh-spoken. There was something about Oxford and self-employment and a loose association with the arts, but it took some prodding before I was finally able to work out that the most important qualification for being a Fat Boy was that you didn't have to go back to the office after lunch. As Miles commented in a moment of unusual lucidity, "I've always thought if you don't have it done by Friday lunchtime, you're unlikely to get it done by the end of the day anyway."

Overall the explanation had a bit of machismo, chest-beating pride on behalf of the assembled guests, who included a magazine editor, the publisher of a local newspaper, a Fleet Street journalist, two novelists, and a former military man turned vintner. D, in fact, was in the employ of someone else who might reasonably expect to be able to reach him on Friday afternoon but seemed to qualify on the basis of his employer's association with the theater and possibly because we owned a station wagon, which Miles correctly suspected he could persuade me to chauffeur. But all these men shared at least the illusion of being in charge of their own destiny for this particular afternoon, and they were going to spend it drinking copious amounts of booze.

D materialized (having chosen coral cashmere) and, after a case of wine was loaded into the trunk of my car, we were off. The brief journey to the pub was no cause for a respite in gossip. A story about how the ex-wife of one of the Fat Boys had a lover in common with Princess Di—presumably the reason she was now an ex—was my reward for depositing my charges at the door of the pub.

The call to retrieve them came five hours later. When I arrived, they were on whiskey and cognac, and there was no sign of the case of wine. One suede-loafered man was wandering around with a half-empty bottle of port, and the ex-army officer turned winemaker was telling me how he was shocked to learn over lunch that I stripped my way through college to pay the bills. (I was shocked to learn this too.) After an aborted attempt to find a Fat Boy from Suffolk presumed to still be in the pub, I managed to herd them into my car and back to the wine bar where the man from Suffolk had already made his way.

The scene that followed was much as you might expect after a dozen men have spent five hours drinking champagne, beer, red wine, port, cognac, and whiskey. Miles kept falling into a coatrack. His ex-wife, Lillian, did not look amused and was not her same warm, friendly self toward me. I imagined she was horrified D had fallen in with this crew and assumed our marriage was headed for the same eventual destiny as her own. D mistook a request for his last name from a fellow Fat Boy attendee as some kind of insult, then insisted his over-the-top response was meant to be a joke. The man from Suffolk kept telling me his life was a mess—just back after ten years in Japan, freshly divorced and with two kids—none of which made any sense to me because I couldn't shake the idea that he looked exactly like the gay, lecherous Uncle Monty from the film *Withnail and I*.

It seemed best to dissociate myself from the Fat Boys, so I mingled. The most amusing of my new acquaintances was a portly man of about sixty who was a good six inches shorter than I am, and had thick, black-rimmed glasses on a cord, a set of rotten, fence-post teeth, and a cut-glass accent. When I asked him what he did, he said, "My dear, I own Farmington," the village up the hill from us. Twice he told me I had a very red nose, which is true, and twice that he'd just as soon comment on my figure as my nose, but he couldn't see it underneath my coat. Despite his arrogance, I found him entertaining and was half-tempted to drop the coat and strike a pose. All the better that I didn't, seeing that his wife was losing her patience at his refusal to leave the wine bar and go to dinner. His defense was that he wasn't "leaving with a bloody half bottle of wine left." She barked orders at him like he was a naughty dog, which he undoubtedly deserved, and he eventually made his exit. D had apparently had his fill of being a man in charge of his own destiny and offered no resistance when I told him it was time to go, using the age-old lure of sausage, chips, and curry from the Chinese takeout restaurant across the square.

There's an urban legend about the Chinese takeout restaurant that keeps rearing its head, which brings me to the question of whether a rural town can have an urban legend. I will assume for the moment it can.

The legend, like all good legends, involves eccentric aristocrats, but also chow mein. One night years ago, a member of the local landed gentry shuffled into the wine bar. He was wearing velvet slippers, as you do when you are landed gentry. The wine bar was chock-full of Toff-y types who do deference very well, so nobody mentioned the slippers. Indeed they made sure their lord's glass never went empty.

After a while, the aristocrat got hungry and decided he needed Chinese takeout. He shuffled off across the square to order his food, and this is where it all went south. The Chinese restaurant is strictly cash only, but naturally our lord didn't deign to carry the paper stuff on his person. He'd never had a need for it, having "people" who transact on his behalf. The owners of the Chinese restaurant were, however, immune to class distinctions and made no exceptions.

Anticipating this conundrum, Roddy the barman headed across the square to pay the bill. But if the person telling you the story has had a lot of wine, there's a different ending where Roddy doesn't figure at all. In this version, the proprietors of the restaurant brandished a cleaver and chased the lord out the door while the wine bar patrons gaped in horror. A lesson in Chinese democracy, never mind the owners were Malaysian.

Right before Christmas there was time for one final celebration, a lamb roast at Rupert and Ralph's flat during which they confided they, too, had gained weight since they started weekending in the country. It seemed our metabolisms, starved of urban stress and toil, had gone into hibernation. Folds of flesh now revealed themselves at the slightest bend, and, when I sat, accordion pleats materialized around my torso. I took to grasping my sides and kneading them as I attempted to locate ribs, kind of like that piano song where you roll your knuckles back and forth across the black keys. It's as if I was still convincing myself that, yes, I was now quite fat. Who needed a pregnancy for that?

In any case, diets and further consideration of motherhood could wait. We were celebrating that I had passed my driving test on the first try, much to D's surprise and in spite of the fact that my driving instructor was fired by the Automobile Association the day before, as it turns out for threatening to "thump" another instructor, not his teaching skills. I would need the driver's license, as I had accepted the job I had been offered and started in the new year.

Checkpoint Charlie
with Palm Trees

CHRISTMAS VACATION was a repeat of the previous year, a week with my parents in Florida. After initially resisting the ritualistic British winter flight to the sun, I have now fully embraced it as fundamental to my health. I am finally able to appreciate Florida, a state I spent much of adolescence plotting to flee, including unsuccessfully lobbying my parents to send me away to boarding school.

We have a routine when visiting my parents. It starts each morning with a jog around the neighborhood, which consists of a mazelike series of gated communities with names like Mystic Ridge and Heron Glen nested within the larger security-guarded compound of Pelican Landing. The Colony is the most exclusive and ultimate lockdown subcommunity within Pelican Landing. It has its own separate golf course, country club, and security guards, who once turned my mother back as she attempted to breech the perimeter on her beach cruiser bicycle. It's like Checkpoint Charlie with palm trees.

After jogging, we head to Bonita Beach for a couple of hours of sun, using the aging Toyota Avalon my father lends us for the week. I try to ignore the NRA and Stop Socialism bumper stickers and be thankful for not having to rent a car. If I've forgotten my bathing suit in London, I can always wear the twenty-year-old faded purple-and-neon-pink paisley bikini that, through the dual miracle of American residential storage space and worn-out elastic, still resides in the upstairs-bathroom drawer and still stretches to fit. Lying on the beach listening to the radio from Doc's Beach House blare out "Send Her My Love," "The Time of My Life," and a synthesizer version of "Deck the Halls," it feels like nothing has really changed from my high school days other than some extra bulges and my willingness to spend $15.90 to rent a chaise lounge so sand doesn't get in my bathing suit.

With all this beach time, I work my way through my vacation reading material much faster than anticipated. *The New Yorker* fiction issue will be consumed cover to cover bar the financial page, as will my novel. Even my mother's *Bon Appétit,* thanks to which I will be familiar with the eating habits of Ryan Seacrest, will be picked clean, leaving me with silent contemplation set to the lapping waves of the Gulf of Mexico.

Like a toddler who prefers the bubble wrap to the fancy toy that came in it, expatriates find Taco Bell and Target to be two of the chief pleasures of returning to the States. Lunch at Taco Bell—cheap and Mexican, both rare in England—happens before or after the beach, depending on how early a start we get. Then the afternoon is spent on what D calls a "spot of retail therapy." (It's okay when this phrase is used in a lifestyle magazine but somehow wrong when it comes out of his mouth.) At Target, we routinely have to perform interventions with one another to prevent regrettable choices, like the time D had to pry the large black leatherlike tote with lots of shiny hardware and a sticky zipper out of my hands in the checkout line. I enter a delusional state brought on by the prices, even at diminished exchange rates, and, in this case, had convinced myself the purse was a Birkin Bag–esque steal. I was not successful in stopping him from purchasing the half-size-too-small Chukka boots that do admittedly resemble the pair in the gentleman's clothier in Cirencester.

After shopping, it's dinner with my parents at a chain restaurant in one of the infinite new strip malls. My parents only eat at three restaurants, Bone Fish Grill, Carraba's, or, if they're feeling zany, P.F. Chang's China Bistro. (The mock Irish pub has been struck off the list due to the dubious nature of fries served with curry.) The strength of the boundaries to this culinary repertoire became clear, when, on night two, my parents offered to take D out to dinner for a belated birthday meal. He suggested a nice hotel by the water or maybe one of the outdoor restaurants in downtown Naples. We knew from the balking that followed that the invitation was really only good for one of the chain restaurants. We were at Carraba's in time for happy hour two-for-one Pinot Grigio. My father knows all the waitstaff by name, including our server, Tiffany, from whom he not-so-secretly ordered a sundae with a candle. Its delivery was accompanied, inevitably, by the entire waitstaff singing "Happy Birthday to You" in Italian to D.

I've given up on any postdinner, communal-family television watching. The first night I attempted this with an "E! True Hollywood Story" on Oprah. My parents expressed a bizarrely vehement disdain for Oprah, their chief complaint seeming to be a suspicion she doesn't read all the books in her book club. I suspect there's some Obama-related mistrust lurking there too, and I decided if we couldn't agree on Oprah, there was really no use trying with anything else.

To be fair, D and I had brought this uneasy situation on ourselves with that fateful, ill-advised decision to tell them last Christmas that we were going to "try." For most of the year, I managed to avoid any further discussion with them on the topic, other than the occasional tentative yet hopeful inquiry from my mother. These were usually couched in cringeworthy language, like when D emailed my parents a press release about his job and my mother responded with a single line: "Any junior executives on the way?"

About three days into our holiday stay with my parents, I had given nothing further away on the topic, and the guilt was starting to get to me. This was affecting my enjoyment of important American vacation activities like Taco Bell quesadilla consumption, so that night over dinner, I broached the topic. We were at my parents' favorite of their three chain restaurants, the Bone Fish Grill, which is more crowded and noisy than the average franchise and, therefore, I thought, offered some shelter from the potential fallout of my news. I had agreed with D that my tactic would be to tell them we had been trying but nothing had happened, which strictly speaking was true, if you count the occasional times when I missed a pill and we had sex anyway.

Sure, a part of me felt like the audacious and callous liar I was, toying with my parents' emotions like this. But then I thought of my father. He is a man who thinks not wanting to have children is an unspeakable character defect. Neither is he known for his sensitivity in dealing with life's more delicate issues. Next I thought of my mother and the crushing weight of her expectations. Each passing year seems to bring more grandchildren for her friends, more matching Burberry pinafore and hat sets to buy for a child that is not related to her, more Christmas cards oozing babies not to be found on her own holiday greetings, and further social anxiety about her failure to join the grandmother ranks.

My parents seemed to take the news well, if a bit confused. My father responded first.

"Whatever you want to do is fine by us. We'd be thrilled to have grandchildren, but it's up to you."

Okay, I thought, this is going all right. He seemed calm, levelheaded, practically philosophical by the standards of normal conversation with him. Then it dawned on me he seemed to be responding to different news than I had delivered. He was responding as if I'd told him we'd changed our mind and weren't going to have kids after all.

Rather than leaving this alone like any sane person, I, perhaps empowered by my happy hour sparkling California wine—selected explicitly to demonstrate to my father I was not a selfish DINKy who quaffs champagne—felt genuine indignation on behalf of the imaginary woman I'd just impersonated, delivering news to her parents that she was having trouble conceiving. I mean if what I'd said was actually true, his response would be almost cruel.

"You did hear what I just said?" I blurted out. Then, just to dig the hole deeper, "We are trying."

My mother tried now, asking meekly if I'd like to see a fertility specialist.

"No, no, I'd rather consider adoption if it came to that," a statement that fell into the hypothetically true category I'd been dabbling in so recklessly all evening.

I'm not sure how the conversation made the jump from here, but shortly thereafter my husband and my father were in a heated conversation about the fact that we'd never consider having more than one child.

"Well, if you're only going to have one, then don't bother," my father was saying, reeling off lists of reasons why this was cruel and unfair to a child. D was getting more and more animated, his outrage rising as his father-in-law tried to dictate to him the acceptable terms of family. My mother put an end to this just in time for our main courses to arrive.

"I was an only child," she said, making an indignant face at my father. And with that, we retreated into our meals and a truce.

Two nights later, we went to my uncle's house for Christmas Eve dinner. My cousin was there with his wife and three children. His cousin was also there with his wife and three daughters. That cousin has two more grown daughters from a first marriage, and his current wife was now visibly pregnant with what would be his sixth child. The current wife was quick to tell us it was a surprise. Her face said mistake.

My uncle has a miniranch, with horses, Texas longhorn cattle he raises for fun, a handful of near-tame goats, three dogs, and a selection of barnyard cats. The kids were in their element in this, their own private petting zoo. While my uncle took them all on a riding mower–drawn hay ride, the other men gathered around the back of my cousin's pickup truck, which contained a large cooler of beer. My cousin was wearing his standard attire, a snap-front, Western-style shirt and Wrangler jeans. His cousin wore a Hawaiian shirt and jeans, and both wore cowboy boots. D wore a loud, pink-striped dress shirt with dark jeans and loafers and held a stemmed glass of white wine. He cleared his throat and prepared to make a valiant effort to join in a conversation about American football. At precisely that moment, the pregnant wife walked by. My father clasped D's shoulder, pointed at her, and said loudly, "That's what you need to do to my daughter."

Part Two: In Residence

New Job, New Nemesis

IN JANUARY, I started my new job, which meant I spent an hour commuting each way through villages with names like Petty France and Old Sodbury. I felt like James Herriot driving through picture-postcard country lanes to that zippy music of the opening credits of *All Creatures Great and Small*. Thankfully, my car was more airtight than his old jalopy, useful since it was below freezing that entire first week. After the snow melted there was a true frost. The entire landscape looked like it had been sugar-dipped. It was something I'd never seen before, having grown up in Florida where frost refers to that one night a year when farmers worry the orange crop might be lost and houses with showpiece fireplaces light up an instamatic log. It was so cold I crafted a special outfit for evenings around our drafty cottage: black imitation Ugg boots, pale pink Chinese silk pajama pants, nubby oatmeal sweater with protruding long-sleeve orange T-shirt, all topped with a glen plaid L.L. Bean bathrobe. I looked like a hobo who had stolen a Russian dancer costume from a cut-rate production of *The Nutcracker*.

Sartorial issues aside, while I was settling beautifully into country life, D was taking it less well. His exact words to me within twenty-four hours of returning to England from Florida in early January were, at volume, "You've ruined it."

By which he meant, I'd ruined his concept of our rural idyll. The Cotswolds was no longer the joyous place where we arrived together each Thursday night for the weekend, our worldly cares evaporating as we left urban grit behind and rolled past open landscapes, starry skies, and stone cottages into the market square where the wine bar sat waiting for us with convivial conversation, a roaring fire, and glass or three of wine. It was now the place where I lived, littered with the detritus of daily life like dishes in the sink and half-read magazines. I was careful to minimize such evidence before D showed up for the first time since I'd permanently moved into the cottage, but he could imagine it and that was enough.

He didn't seem to remember that this was all his idea in the first place. Gone was any recollection of the way he had tarted up that dull job in Swindon. Back then, he was a used-car salesman touting its merits. But his brain didn't seem to make the logical connection that if I got a job near the Cotswolds, only I would be living here full-time. Now he understood. I lived in the beautiful countryside all the time. I was the enemy. Given this and my new special cold weather outfit, it was probably a good thing for our marriage that he wasn't going to be around much during the week.

Luckily for me, D soon found another person to hate. He had a new boss, who coincidentally used to work with me at my former London job. The new boss was a music industry big shot, French, and known to occasionally have a silent conversation with my chest in the elevator. This last fact was known to D but was not the reason the new boss, whom we nicknamed Inspector Clouseau, had become his nemesis. D just doesn't like having a boss, and prior to Inspector Clouseau he had a boss in name rather than practice. I was no longer persona non grata numero uno, but D's resentment toward me still grew because I was unavailable in person two nights a week for him to complain about the Inspector.

Still the Inspector absorbed enough of the heat usually saved for me that I could safely share with D some insight into the loveliness of my new weekly rural routine. There was the gym I joined in Cirencester, or "Siren, as we locals call it," I explained to him. It's run by the local council but nicer and cheaper than any private gym I had been to in London, and you could park for free! (Living in London had clearly warped my sense of what it was appropriate to get excited about.) Each Thursday, a milk float made deliveries to the front door, and, most Tuesday nights, Lillian brought eggs from her flock of hens to the wine bar, £1 for a half dozen. With these amenities, it's no wonder people lived in Gloucestershire. It was a no-brainer, the same way homeless people gravitate to our former hometown of Santa Monica. I couldn't believe I ever lived in London. I thought this last bit rather than saying it out loud to D.

In his exasperation, D put the London flat on the rental market, toying with the idea that he could join me in the full-time country life while retaining his London job. This would mean about four hours of daily commute time assuming all went smoothly, and with the recession in full swing and the rental market sagging, the plan seemed optimistic. There are, in fairness, gentlemen of a certain means who regularly commute into London from Gloucestershire. I had seen them on the railway platform with their laptop bags and velvet-collared coats on the odd morning in the last year when I had taken the train into London for work. But I suspect most of them have a pied-à-terre in London to accommodate train cancellations, bad weather, and the occasional night out in the city. At six hundred square feet, we essentially had a pied-à-terre in London; the mortgage just cost about twice as much as the one in the country, which took the charm out of having property with a French nickname. We may have had a house in Poshtershire, but we were several salary zeros away from those commuting gents.

At the end of January, we got a call from the realtor who had listed our London flat for rental. She had an offer from an Italian couple moving over to England to work. It was slightly less per month than what we wanted, which made it easy. I said no, thinking the matter was closed. The next day, the realtor called back: The Italians would meet our price. We thought about it. We debated the pros and cons and did the math, all day, all night, and part of the next day. It turned out the cost of the monthly train ticket D would need to commute from the Cotswolds was fully half of our monthly mortgage on the London flat, which meant there was a lot of potential commuting aggravation without that much financial benefit in consolidating homes. I told D it was his decision, and he turned the offer down. The Italians must have thought we were playing hard to get because the realtor came back with an offer over our asking price. D apologized, said no, and took the flat off the market. For the time being, he was still a weekender and we still had a London flat. Make that a pied-à-terre.

Communion

M Y PATIENCE COLLAPSED over a trivial incident, as is always the case, one Sunday morning. While driving to church, I nearly missed a turn despite having driven this route a hundred times before.

"Where did you think you were going?" D asked twice for good measure.

"Fuck off. It was a mistake, I make them," I replied at volume.

We exchanged no other words until after the Prayers of Penitence. D nudged me. Softened by prayers admitting what asses we all are, I assumed he was, too, and expected an apology, or at least a smile that implied as much. Instead I was told off in hushed tones for wearing my gloves inside the church. It's cold in this old stone church. And it's not exactly formal. A black lab snoozed at the feet of the elderly occupants of the pew in front of us, and the gloves stayed on.

Then Godfrey opened his sermon with a prayer from Mother Teresa:

> *Though you hide yourself behind the unattractive disguise of the irritable, the exacting, the unreasonable, may I still recognize you and say Jesus, my patient, how sweet it is to serve you.*

The irritable, the exacting, the unreasonable. Interesting. I always associated Mother Teresa with lepers, but she also seems to have spent time with my husband. My fuming continued unabated during the Prayers of Intercession that followed. I prayed shamelessly for me, me, me, not Iraq or Afghanistan or the bloody queen, as Dorothy implored us to do.

Next up was communion, which I usually sit out for a variety of reasons, the main one being that it's all about the crucifixion, the heart of what separates Christianity from other religions. And that separation, that thing that makes people feel special or different or better than, is the thing I dislike about religion. (Whether it's the three precepts or the five pillars or the Ten Commandments, the major world religions have more in common than not, and I'd prefer to focus on that.) Then there's the hygiene issue of all those people drinking out of the same glass. And finally there's the technically correct and less controversial reason I gave the vicar when he asked me last month why I abstained. I'm not confirmed in the Church of England, so I assumed it wasn't kosher, so to speak. He assured me it wasn't an issue.

As the half of the tiny congregation on my side of the aisle filed up to the altar, Dorothy, sitting in the pew opposite, looked me in the eye and said, "He said you should come."

"What?" I replied, despite having heard exactly what she said.

"He said you should come," she repeated, leaning over and clasping my arm.

Dorothy had clearly overheard my previous conversation with the vicar. But for a brief moment in my vulnerable state I thought the "he" in her mandate was God on some kind of direct line to her with advice for the pouting woman across the aisle.

And so I did what I had been told to do and made my way up to the railing where I knelt and waited. Godfrey deposited a wafer into my open palm—it had seemed right to remove my gloves for this. Jean, the lay minister, followed offering a sip of port from the silver chalice, enough to dislodge the

Styrofoam disc now stuck to the roof of my mouth. Both spoke softly and directly to each participant: the body of Christ, the blood of Christ. This wasn't the self-service communion of my Presbyterian childhood, where large gold trays holding plastic shot glasses of grape juice and stale torn bread were passed around. This was different. It felt like being ministered to, which is exactly what I needed.

Field Guide Number Three:

Walk for bickering against a scenic backdrop on a fine day

Distance	8 miles (approximately)
Duration	If you are walking with your partner, allow half a day for this ramble. If your walking group consists of women only, you can slice off an hour thanks to your intuitive sense of and ability to ask for directions. If your walking group is all male, best not to make any plans for the rest of the day and do remember to bring a GPS-enabled cell phone.
Difficulty	Moderate with some steep sections, especially if you accidentally veer off the path

Here's one of my favorite rambles/ways to fight with my husband, starting and finishing in the lovely village of Snowshill. Snowshill is that rare thing in the Cotswolds, a village with a name that sounds as picturesque as it really is. Other Cotswold villages are laden with less charming names. Upper and Lower Slaughter come to mind, as do Northleach, Eastleach, and Lechlade, which together form a triumvirate evocative of leeches and lecherousness.

1. We start where we intend to finish: the pub. After fortifying yourself with a ploughman's lunch at the Snowshill Arms, head left out of the pub and walk along the road past Snowshill Manor, now a National Trust property open to the public. If you've started to fight with your partner over directions at this point in the walk, it may be best to cut your losses and just pay a visit to the Manor or the lavender farm farther up the road.

2. Beyond the parking lot, there is a stile and signpost for a public path on the left-hand side of the road. Follow it through the sheep field and down into the valley. Cross the stream and follow the path up the other side of the valley until you reach a dirt road running parallel to the woods. Take a right, which will be the last time that day your partner and you agree on the route, and follow it along the woods until it starts to curve around to the left.

3. Here you will have some choices, the clearest of which would be to join the well-delineated Cotswold Way just off to your right. You may find, however, that your partner would rather argue about whether or not it is necessary to cross a field of bulls in order to progress to Stanton, throwing his or her Ordnance Survey map to the ground and accusing you of being antagonistic in the process. Best just to smile calmly in the face of this sort of behavior and wait for the tantrum to pass before starting to make

slow but firm progress in the direction of the Cotswold Way (which yes, I know, is where you suggested you head all along). You'll have a good stretch of tense silence along the Cotswold Way, punctuated by the occasional outburst that causes other fellow ramblers to hang back. This is okay, as asking them for directions at this point would be deemed further proof of your "antagonism."

4. After a while, you'll reach a crossroads where, if you're lucky, a pink-nosed, fluffy lamb will have broken loose from the adjoining pasture. This will give your partner a chance to rescue it before it succeeds in strangling itself by head-butting the wire fencing in its futile attempts to get back to mama ewe. Your partner's ensuing feelings of heroism will help defuse any lingering resentment toward you for having a good sense of direction. Pointing out that any old fool could see where to go just by using Broadway Tower as a landmark is not advised at this juncture, as it would jeopardize your credibility when it came to influencing the decision to go right and continue on the Cotswold Way into Stanton.

5. This is a lovely leg of the journey, where near-tame, chocolate-colored cows swirl around you on the path. Careful, though. In your state of bucolic bliss, you may impulsively suggest a shortcut that takes you off the Cotswold Way, through some woods, and down a muddy, precipitous decline into Stanton. You'll soon know you're in Stanton when you arrive at a little triangle of a green with a ceremonial coach light hanging from a wooden post. The church is to the left, and the pub is to the right. Naturally, you should head right.

6. The Mount Inn delivers panoramic views from its two patio areas. Enjoy some refreshment before heading up and out on the path just behind and to the left of the pub. The route out

is more efficient than the improvised route in, and within
twenty minutes, you'll be back to the site of Operation Lamb
Rescue. This will stir up good memories in your partner so
that he or she is susceptible to your final route alteration
(my, you're brave), which takes you off the Cotswold Way
via some National Trust signposted woods. Soon you'll be in
another sheep field, then head right on the road all the way
back into Snowshill. The pub may yet be open for evening
service, but check around back and the barmaid may just
serve you a pint of SBA and a ginger beer to enjoy in the
garden, as she did for us.

Cockaleekie, Neeps, and Tatties

THE HIGHLIGHT of that January was the two-hundred-fiftieth-anniversary Burns Night dinner. There is something quintessentially British about a celebration that includes haggis, sheep stomach lining stuffed with bits of offal, as its culinary centerpiece. It is also a measure of how desperately the populace needs something to look forward to in January, the bleakest month. Yet at the same time, I have to admire a country that turns out each year in full bagpipe- and family-tartan regalia to celebrate a long-dead poet. D attempted to diminish this by pointing out that his fellow countrymen will use any excuse for a "piss up." Still I think it's a nice idea. Perhaps the United States could come up with its own annual drunken celebration of a poet; Bukowski day seems fitting.

We attended the Burns Night celebrations in the pub one village over with Rupert and Ralph. The venue was a tactical decision based on the availability of a vegetarian haggis option, a requirement for D, not because he is a vegetarian but because he is opposed to organ meat of any variety. The meal started with the recitation of a Burns poem, during which the slick, shot-put-sized disc of haggis—easily mistaken for a gray Jell-O mold—was sliced open with great pomp and circumstance to the accompaniment of bagpipes, or in our case, a CD of The Red Hot Chili Pipers. I am still not sure what it means—I'm one of those people who

needed subtitles to watch *Trainspotting*—but the cue for making
the ceremonial cut is vivid:

> *Trenching your gushing entrails bright*
> *Like onie ditch;*
> *And then, O what a glorious sight,*
> *Warm-reekin, rich!*

Unlike D, I went for the real thing, which arrived following
our cockaleekie (chicken and leek) soup and was accompanied
by neeps and tatties (parsnips and mashed potatoes). It was half-
school-cafeteria mystery meat, half-spicy-veggie burger. Everyone
who had eaten haggis before claimed it was the best they'd ever had,
with a surprisingly pleasant firmness to it. It disturbed me that we
had lapsed into discussing our meal in the language of bowel move-
ments, but a nightcap of a wee dram helped distract me.

The low point of January came early one Sunday night when I
called Dynasty Cantonese Cuisine, the legendary Chinese takeout restaurant housed in a little freestanding stone building in the
market square. The phone rang and rang. No answer. They must
be too busy to pick up. I persuaded D to bundle up and accompany me on the block-long walk to place our order in person. This
is when we first noticed the sign:

> *We are closed until further notice. We apologise for any*
> *inconvenience caused.*
> —the management

We were disappointed. There was no food—well no food we
wanted to eat—in the fridge, which led to the accusation from D
that I lacked ambition when it comes to regular grocery shopping,
something he claimed had worsened since I had moved full-time
to the country. We retreated into the comforts of a new season of
American Idol and cheese toast, my trusty standby dinner.

Another week passed, and the sign remained. Theories abounded.

"They're just on holiday. They went away last year this time for a few weeks. They'll be back."

Or "Probably just some trouble with Immigration. They'll be back."

Every theory ended with "They'll be back." I was skeptical. If the owners were going on vacation why not just say so? Vacations end on a date, not "until further notice." The sign was ominous.

January came to a close and the Chinese restaurant failed to open. Panic started to spread in the village. People who had been known to snobbishly refer to Dynasty as "Die Nasty" looked thin and stricken. Toff and townie alike mourned the loss of barbequed spareribs and fries on demand, french fries being a legitimate rice substitute in British Chinese restaurants. (According to my chief trivia source at the wine bar, we owe this phenomenon to Billy Butlin, the founder of Butlins holiday camps that had their British heyday in the 1950s and '60s—think the Adirondacks resort in *Dirty Dancing*. Mr. Butlin was a fan of Chinese food and decided to introduce it at his holiday camps but served it with fries to ease the public into appreciating this exotic new cuisine. Ever since, the British consumer has demanded nothing less.)

There was a brief period last year when I swore off Chinese food. I found that a bottle of Gamay finished off with a 10:00 PM meal of prawn toast, veggie chow mein, and Kung Pao chicken invariably resulted in me waking with a start at 2:00 AM, eyes wide and heart pounding, fueled by the sugar and sodium bomb my body was attempting to digest. But by and large, Chinese food holds a special place in my heart. It's been with us since the beginning of our Cotswold adventure when we used to arrive in the village on a Friday night. We'd natter over a glass in the wine bar with Roddy, while waiting for our takeout feast to be readied. And it's rescued us on occasion when guests have come to visit and somehow the dinner reservation was missed because another bottle of Prosecco at the wine bar seemed like a good idea. It's even been the epicenter of village intrigue and scandal, including a rumored drug bust (apparently they have those in the Cotswolds too).

The charm of Dynasty was its anticharm. (After all, a Chinese takeout restaurant in the middle of a Cotswold town square doesn't exactly ooze charm in the manner of, say, a timber-beamed pub.) It was a brusque, efficient, cash-only kind of place manned by a steely faced, thirty-something Malaysian couple. The wife, a slight woman forever in an oversized T-shirt and baseball cap, ran front of house from behind a tall counter. Decoration was sparse, consisting of some peeling wallpaper dotted with gold Chinese characters, an oversized calendar, and a shelf displaying cans of soda on offer. I'm not sure if there really was a large waving ceramic cat on the counter or if I've just imagined that. Her husband fired the food in the kitchen behind, which was separated by a doorway that was hung with a limp plastic shower curtain liner cut in half. That day's *Sun* newspaper was always on the front counter to provide entertainment while waiting for your food, which was just as well since conversation with the woman was hard work. Once, feeling chatty after a few glasses of wine, I thought I'd managed to forge a bond by coaxing out of her that she was from Kuala Lumpur, a city where I had also briefly lived some years ago. After that, I was convinced she had started to give me free prawn crackers until I realized everyone who spent £15 or more got them.

Now February had drawn to a close, the ominous sign remained in the window, and the door was still locked. Around the village, the mourning process moved from denial to acceptance. Good-bye, Dynasty. You fed us well. You will be missed.

Sunday Lunch

IN MARCH, we had lunch. It wasn't just any lunch. It was Sunday lunch, a fixture of English life, and a ritual I had admired since we first moved to London. There it was an event that played out in pubs, where groups of friends would arrive with armfuls of newspapers. I used to look in at them through the windows of our corner pub, The Bonaparte, with their steaming plates of roast beef and Yorkshire pudding and all those papers spread around like they were getting ready to paint something. The closest thing I could think of to this routine in Los Angeles was aspiring actors/directors/screenwriters sitting at a coffee shop gripping a soy chai latte in one hand and a script in the other. The harder the person tried to look nonchalant, the more deliberate the whole thing seemed. The English version seemed both gastronomically and intellectually superior. And now we had been invited to Sunday lunch, the first since our arrival in the Cotswolds.

This one was a belated birthday celebration for Miles and was hosted by his ex-wife, Lillian. (Fraternizing between ex-spouses is uncommonly common in the Cotswolds, presumably a coping mechanism for divorcees to maintain a social life in such a small community). Like all good parties, this one took place largely in her kitchen around the farmhouse table. After pheasant pie and potatoes Dauphinoise but before almond cake and coffee, snowflakes started dancing outside the kitchen window, which was already framing a picture-perfect winter-white landscape. I was pretty sure Hugh Grant and Emma Thompson were about to walk through the door and join us for the cheese course.

An entire cast of Richard Curtis characters wouldn't have been more interesting than the assembled company. In addition to the charms of Miles and his ex, we were joined by another couple. The husband, also one of the Fat Boys, resembled Paul Bunyan in his leather waistcoat and is a writer whose work I knew from my favorite newspaper. These facts alone would have been enough to sustain me for the entire afternoon, but he turned out to be only too happy to further oblige my stereotype of an idiosyncratic former Fleet Street journalist. While the rest of the table drank rioja, he steadily drained the bottle of The Famous Grouse and a small pitcher of water that had been set out at his place. (This is the only manner in which I have seen water offered at a Cotswold table. Unless it's accompanying whiskey, locals seem to think using water to hydrate yourself is somehow wimpy.) Between courses, he smoked hand-rolled cigarettes and told me stories about his early years in Los Angeles and New York.

Neither did his wife disappoint. She was dressed in Toff I-don't-give-a-shit, in this case a ripped hot-pink cashmere V-neck, jeans, and leopard-print loafers. I think it was my compliment of her ring—Fabergé—that sparked the conversation that revealed her father had been a Pulitzer Prize–winning journalist who, while stationed in the AP's Moscow bureau during the Stalin era, eloped with her mother, a ballerina in The Bolshoi. Clark Gable played her father in the film version of her parents' romance. Really.

I couldn't help feeling a little bit sorry for her. How are you ever supposed to live up to parents like that? It was enough to make me grateful for my own parents' relative mediocrity. The day before on a phone call with my father I had to explain to him what cava was. He seemed downright fascinated to learn about the existence of this economically priced Spanish sparkling wine.

"How do you know about things like that?" he asked, his voice filled with genuine wonder.

On second thought, my father may have just been expressing understandable bafflement that my knowledge of wine seemed to eclipse my knowledge of the birds and the bees. Or at least my seeming ability to act on it.

Citizen

NOT LONG AFTER that Sunday lunch, I tried on a jacket at Pakeman Catto & Carter, a gentlemen's and ladies' clothier in Cirencester, housed in a three-story townhouse that's all polished wood, glass cases, and claret carpets. The jacket was a tailored number made of green tweed with a coral-colored windowpane overlay and sage-silk lining. It was handsome, half-price, and fit me like a glove according to the sales assistant, who called me madam and asked me to spin around as he assessed the length and shoulders. It was, he informed me, a hacking jacket, another one of those cryptic horsey terms so prolific around the Cotswolds, like "on the gallops" or "a jolly." D was equally as admiring, fitting as this did his aspirational vision of our conversion to Toffdom.

The only previous time in my life where I would have fit in without note while wearing a tweed hacking jacket was at Camp Merrie Woode, the all-girls camp in Sapphire, North Carolina that specialized in paddling and equestrian sports and where I spent three summers between the ages of twelve and fourteen. The camp uniform consisted of forest-green shorts and a gray sailor smock with a matching green tie. I felt like a Martian when I showed up fresh from south Florida with my trio of skinny neon belts and heart-bedecked Vans slip-ons to accessorize what I thought of as the hopelessly unstylish attire I was expected to wear day in and day out for the next three weeks. (In my defense, this was the 1980s.) The other girls, girls with names like Darnell and Eleanor from Vermont and Maine, wore L.L. Bean moccasins or plain white Tretorn sneakers, styles that hadn't changed since their mothers had worn them.

The second summer I showed up with a pair of Tretorns, but in an attempt to maintain some style integrity, mine had a madras plaid "V" rather than plain white. I also brought my beloved pump-spray bottle of Aqua Net—aerosol was my preference but strictly forbidden by camp rules—with which to cement my proud poof of feathered bangs, only to have it diluted with water in a prank by my evil cabinmate, Kren, an aspiring thespian who got the lead in the camp production of *The Mikado* while my flat bangs and I were relegated to the chorus. That summer, I was permanently turned off of horseback riding when I was forced to muck out a stall, a mandatory part of our equestrian curriculum. It was difficult to keep my pastel polka-dot driving cap on my head while I scraped shit and mud out of a temperamental horse's hoof with a hook, but I persevered. Someone around there had to stand up for fashion.

At the end of the third summer, I cried when I saw my father waiting for me as I got off the plane. When he asked why I was crying, I was too embarrassed to tell the truth, so I told him it was because I was so sad to have left camp. The truth was I was overwhelmed with relief to be home, away from the freaky canoe and equestrian young people and back amongst teenagers who had the good sense to fawn over my prized pink ankle boots, the pair that made me feel like I had a shot at going steady with Simon Le Bon when I wore them.

Back in Cirencester, I admired myself in the mirror, then hung the hacking jacket back on the sales rack. Wearing it somehow felt disingenuous. It was a beautiful jacket for someone else.

Despite my reluctance to fully adopt the native costume of the Cotswolds, I was proceeding with my application for British citizenship, having recently met the spousal residency requirement. I was not renouncing my American citizenship, rather becoming a dual citizen. It amounted to an elaborate ruse to avoid having to fill in a landing card and stand in the inevitably longer, non-EU passport-holders line at Heathrow. (That, and the fact that British citizenship would make me eligible to work in Europe—Paris, specifically because in my fantasy life that doesn't mean I need to speak French.) It had been months since I parted with the £600, lengthy application, and stack of old utility bills required to apply for citizenship. I hadn't thought much about what becoming a British citizen actually meant until the week when the ceremony in which I would swear my allegiance to HRM the Queen was going to take place.

That's when the doubts set in. Had I earned the right to be a loyal subject in this fair land? Was being too lazy to fill out a landing card a worthy cause? It hardly inspired comparison to Ellis Island, aside from the huddled masses at Heathrow passport control. To make matters more complicated, America was on the up. Sure, the economy was in the pits, but so was the UK's. Obama was starting to restore our country's reputation abroad, the dollar was up, and the pound was down. While I would still be an American, even going "dual" felt like a betrayal. It was like I got separated and now I was getting remarried without getting divorced... which made me a crazy Mormon bigamist. I was confused.

To sort things out, I sat down and made another one of my lists. This one detailed why I deserved to be a British citizen in addition to remaining a proud, if not exactly flag-waving, American:

1. I am proficient in British. Specifically I am totally au fait with the nouns; "boot" and "bin" tumble from my lips on a regular basis. Adjectives are a bit of a stretch. "Bloody" still doesn't sound right coming out, but I did ask someone if he was "cross" the other night without so much as a pause. Verbs are fewer in general. Most are some variation of hooking up—to "shag," to "pull," to "cop off"—and then, in my eighth year of marriage, I had limited use for such vocabulary. I have been known to "fancy" something, as

in "I fancy an Indian tonight," by which I mean a curry dinner, not shagging an Indian man.

2. I have made a genuine effort to fit in. My lean Los Angeles limbs have morphed to a pie-filled pear shape. My perfectly aligned teeth used to practically taunt "my dentistry is better than yours," but now, with increased tea consumption, have mellowed to a less ostentatious gleam.

3. I am addicted to *The Archers,* an agricultural soap opera and Radio 4 institution. Imagine if *The Guiding Light* never made the leap to television and was set completely on a farm. Recent dialogue in an episode featuring a lambing scene included, "This one's cervix isn't dilated. Where's the lubricant?"

I used to hate *The Archers,* whose chirpy opening ditty seemed to start up every time I turned on the radio on a long car trip. Now I loved it, perhaps coaxed into its grip by a regular car commute and country life. But reasons didn't matter. My change of heart was the equivalent of developing a taste for Marmite, certain proof I was worthy of calling myself a Brit.

The citizenship ceremony took place at three o'clock in the afternoon on a Thursday in the Gloucester registrar office, which sits on the edge of the town center of the Gloucestershire county seat. To describe the building's large sash windows with mauve trim or the front portico's three plaster-wreath-topped columns makes it sound much grander than it is. Inside there are fussy window treatments and silk floral arrangements to acknowledge the significance of the civil ceremonies taking place in its rooms. But these comingle with relics from the early eighties—abstract-patterned ceiling tiles, green carpet, cheap wood-paneled walls—to create an unmistakable municipal effect.

Still the letter from the Home Office inviting me to attend left me some hope in the department of pomp and circumstance, promising as it did that a representative of HRM Queen Elizabeth II would be in attendance. This turned out to be one Major M. T. N. H. Wills, the deputy lord lieutenant of Gloucestershire, whose name I recognized because his family owns most of the land around our Cotswold village, known simply as the Wills estate. Major Wills wore a gray morning coat and a matching waistcoat and trousers with his comb-over. Add a top hat and he could have been on his way to Ladies' Day at Royal Ascot.

My fellow citizens-to-be didn't exactly look ready for Ascot, but they had made a good effort. The mother of what I guessed to be an Ethiopian family was in a dark purple suit with rhinestone and pearl drop earrings, and curly bangs tinted the same color as her suit. An Indian man in a crisp gray suit and pink tie was accompanied by a male friend wielding an expensive-looking digital camera. A little Chinese girl twirled in her classic little party dress of cap sleeves, wide sash, and full skirt with patent-leather Mary Janes. (The thought did cross my mind that perhaps I could interest her family in reopening a well-trafficked and recently defunct Chinese restaurant in our village.) Even the fully covered Muslim woman managed a headscarf edged with rhinestones. I was straight from work and dressed in black boots, black tights, a black skirt, and a black wool-jersey shirt brightened up with a splash of charcoal gray. I felt both self-conscious and crass since my main concern up until then was to get this show on the road; I only had enough change for an hour from the pay-and-display parking machine. Now a part of me regretted not asking D to take the afternoon off work to accompany me. This suddenly felt like the kind of thing we should have taken more seriously.

As we all sat waiting for the ceremony to begin, a CD player boomed rousing classical music by English composers of the "Dam Busters March" and Elgar ilk. To add further ambiance, there was a large framed photograph of the Queen propped on a pedestal draped with purple silk. After a few minutes, the registrar began by introducing Major Wills and informing us that after the ceremony, our designated dignitary would be happy to pose for pictures with us. Major Wills did not look like he would be happy to pose for pictures.

The major then stood and slipped on a pair of glasses before reading from a prepared statement about the glories of Gloucestershire—the countryside, the fine market towns, the soaring wool-money cathedrals—and how wise we all were to have chosen to settle here. I couldn't help feeling a swell of pride. The registrar walked around the room and one by one we stood to take our oath. Then Major Wills called us up and presented our naturalization certificates, shook our hand, and directed us over to sign the register. It was over quickly and the new citizens were soon clamoring to take up the registrar's offer for pictures with the major. I considered getting a snap on my phone for fun but was too sheepish. Instead I slipped out the door where a smiling lady from the registrar's office offered me a cup of celebratory coffee or tea. I declined but asked for a cookie to go. She looked at me quizzically.

"I'll have a biscuit," I said, correcting myself and receiving for my efforts a napkin-wrapped chocolate digestive. As I left, I commended myself for choosing well in becoming a citizen of a country that shamelessly disguises cookies in the vocabulary of gastrointestinal health aids. I also knew I would need the sustenance: Spring was looming, and with it the social calendar was starting to pick up.

The Ball

SPRING STARTED with another hunt auction, this time at the invitation of Miles. We didn't know until we arrived at the town hall later that evening that the entrepreneurial Georgina the bird plucker was his considerably younger date. (When I had earlier envied her simple country life, I hadn't taken the perils of village dating into consideration.) I couldn't help thinking this was bound to end in tears, but I was too distracted by the assembled company to let my judgments get the best of me. This included an Austrian count who was tall and pointy, as an Austrian count should be, and seemed to have donated every other lot in the auction. There was also a ginger-haired man of indeterminate age who specialized in horse-breeding data. He was like a Wall Street analyst of the horsey set, researching equine bloodstocks instead of equities.

When it came time to bid, D came close on a lot for a day's gate shutting, presumably a useful service when you ride horses across the vast plot of land that makes up your family's estate and you don't want to get off your horse continually to close gates. The lot didn't specify where said gate shutting was to take place, and D and Miles thought it would be funny to have the donating family come up to London and spend the day closing front gates up and down our road of terraced houses. D bailed at £200, which left him with precisely that amount to purchase a life-coaching session, exactly the kind of namby-pamby, Los Angeles–type thing to ruin one's reputation at an event like this, and the taint by association heaped on our host was exactly what he was going for. It was poor value, considering a week at a villa that sleeps fifteen in the Dordogne went for under a grand.

The real value of the evening came from Georgina, who mentioned in passing that the Hunt Ball the next Saturday was a floor-length-dress-required kind of event. Miles had also invited us to attend that event, and Georgina's news sent me into a mad rush on Sunday, during which I momentarily considered having my mother FedEx me an old bridesmaid dress. It was the only long dress I owned, and in my panic I was prepared to overlook the chiffon and rhinestone scattered flutter sleeves. Presented with this plan, my mother, who just happened to be bruised and bandaged from her most recent bout of plastic surgery (neck and eyes touch-up to her decade-old facelift), shrieked that said dress "looks like a sack" on me. Unlike my mother, the only thing that would be giving me any kind of lift were my Trinny & Susannah Magic Knickers, the British equivalent of Spanx.

The last time I faced this kind of formal-wear emergency imposed by the regulations of British society was a couple of years prior when, two days shy of Ladies' Day at Royal Ascot, I happened to hear mention of the fact that a lady's hat had to cover her entire head to enter the Royal Enclosure. The reasonably priced number I had settled on weeks ago, somewhere between a fascinator—an elaborate feather or bow stuck on a comb—and a beret in scalp coverage, was on the cusp of unacceptable. On a frenzied death march stopping in every milliner within a mile radius of Oxford Street, I parted ways with a considerable sum of money for my now-prized hot-pink, highly feathered pimp hat. If only my evening gown for the hunt ball could be as fabulous.

In the end, I settled for black, which turned out to be a good choice. It was raining hard the night of the ball, but at least the hem of my dress didn't show the mud I dragged in as we crossed the field to the encampment of tents where the event was being held. Inside was indistinguishable from a Park Lane ballroom, except for the seagrass carpet-covered lumpy floor. Waiters circulated with endless champagne, and I kept watch for what I was sure would be some of the finest examples of rural Toffdom's eccentrics and their accompanying outlandish behavior. I was wrong. The most outrageous thing I witnessed all night was a drunken nineteen-year-old who sucked face with her paramour on the dance floor for three consecutive songs. As D is fond of saying, youth are so boring. We were home in bed by 1:30 AM.

Well rested and hangover-free, we made it to church the next morning. We were greeted by the usual suspects, our six elderly ladies and the fiftysomething man who I suspect attends mostly out of civic duty to the golden girls of his village. The upside of a measly church population is everyone gets a job. Jean says matins when Godfrey is tending to another church, the lady who drives her red Nissan Micra like a bat out of hell for the couple of blocks between her cottage and the church reads the Old Testament verse, the lady with the Danish accent takes the New Testament, the gentleman collects the offering and rings the bells, and Dorothy, in her orange peacoat, recites the Collect. This last one is my favorite. Dorothy's prayer reads like an überletter to Santa Claus, her requests ranging from a pony ("good health for the Queen") to a trip to the moon ("peace on earth in our time, Lord"). I say this not to poke fun at her earnest and child-like approach, rather in humble admiration of a person who has managed to retain these qualities after ninety years.

I, on the other hand, am totally godless. That's the only way I can explain why Jean's Lenten sermon made me think of the saga of our local Chinese takeout place. Jean was preaching about when Jesus had to prepare the disciples for the fact he was going to die. They responded with the textbook five stages of grief—denial, anger, bargaining, depression, and acceptance—not unlike my fellow villagers and me when faced with the recent shuttering of Dynasty. But then, just that week, we had been given an early Easter miracle. D, playing the unlikely herald, burst through the back door of the cottage asking if I wanted to hear some fantastic news. He was so jubilant I was sure that Inspector Clouseau had been fired. But no, he brought good tidings that the Dynasty woks were firing once again, like a phoenix risen from the ashes. Just like that, Kung Pao chicken Friday nights were back. I suspect Jean would fail to appreciate my loose interpretation of Easter theology, but it was nearly spring and I was taking my themes of rebirth and renewal where I could find them. I didn't know it yet, but I was going to need them.

Big Head

I HAVE ALWAYS HAD a big head. If a hat label says "one size fits all," I don't even bother trying it on. I need large at a minimum, preferably extra-large. Over the years, there have been both great millinery victories—my Ascot number—and disasters, as when my favorite safari-style summer hat strayed into the clothes dryer and forever out of my life. But in the spring, my brain decided to take the big-head issue to new heights by engaging in what my neurologist termed "a clinically isolated incident of inflammation."

Naturally my first concern was vanity. Upon hearing that the immediate course of treatment for an inflamed brain would be three consecutive days of intravenous steroid treatments, I asked the doctor if there were any side effects, by which, of course, I meant would the steroids make me puffy. What with all the Sunday lunches and the reopening of the Chinese takeout place, I was doing puffy just fine without any extra assistance. It turned out the steroids were anti-inflammatory. So no puffiness was involved, but I am getting ahead of myself.

The whole "incident" started on a Saturday. D and I were out for a bike ride when I commented that I felt like I had marbles in my mouth. This continued over the weekend. With each passing day, I was finding it increasingly hard to speak, ironic given my reputation amongst friends and colleagues as a profligate talker. I felt like a drunk trying hard to sound sober or someone coming off novocaine after a couple of fillings. By lunch hour on Monday,

I knew something was wrong, even though nobody else seemed to notice. I phoned D several times to see if he could hear the slurring, and, despite the fact that he is a devoted hypochondriac when it comes to his own health, he seemed uncertain. When I asked two of my British coworkers with whom I share an office if I sounded funny, they laughed and said only because I was American. Then one asked if I had been drinking and laughed some more.

From there, the week devolved into a series of rapid-fire, process-of-elimination medical appointments aimed at solving the mystery of my degraded speech. On Tuesday afternoon, a general practitioner put me through a drill that seemed a lot like a drunk driving test. After I crossed the room diagonally, toe-to-toe, I checked his face for some indication of how I had performed. He was blank, suspiciously so. I asked him if he was concerned, and he replied that he was concerned enough to send me to an ear, nose, and throat specialist the next day. After a camera was put up my nose to look at my vocal chords and then more coordination tests, the ENT revealed that he had found nothing.

At this point I burst into tears, something I am not prone to do outside of funerals. D and I had privately wondered if I had had a small stroke, and the lack of a logical explanation in the less scary terrain of my ears, nose, or throat tipped me over the edge. I'm not sure if the tears had anything to do with it, but I was swiftly dispatched to the "doughnut," the MRI-scanning machine, and given an appointment with the neurologist for the following Monday. On Thursday, the ENT called me during a break in the operating theater to assure me there were "no tumors or anything like that" but also to let me know he had gotten me in with the head of neurology at six o'clock on Friday. No tumors good, prioritized Friday night neurologist appointment bad.

When I met the neurologist, he had me repeat the whole story and do yet another round of drunk driving tests before he broke the news on my brain scan. I knew there was news to break because he waited for me to tie the laces on the Converse sneakers

I had taken off for the exam before he started to talk. Then out came the "clinically isolated incident" bit. The bad news was that multiple incidents constitute a diagnosis of multiple sclerosis. I asked if multiple meant two, as in if this happened one more time. It did.

Neither D nor I knew anything about MS, so this explanation prompted a barrage of questions, which the neurologist both did and did not answer. We learned MS is a disease that lacks both an explanation and a prognosis; it is more of a name for a collection of symptoms than the promise of cause, calamity, or cure that the word disease implies. And so the discussion turned to my odds of developing this amorphous ailment. These ranged from 50 to 75 percent, depending on what question I asked. It felt like shaking a Magic 8 Ball trying to get the answer you want, only I kept getting "Reply hazy, try again."

To his credit, the neurologist refused to allow D and me to get carried away with what might happen and instead kept us focused on the immediate steroid treatment, which would start the next day. It helped in all this that the doctor, who is tall enough to look like a retired pro basketball player, was calm, gentle, and patient enough for me to wish just a little bit he was my dad. He even made a special trip to see me on Saturday at the hospital when I was getting that first treatment. When the nurse disclosed that he wasn't on duty that day I felt grateful, but concerned that he was so concerned he made the trip on his day off.

The hospital where I was treated was more well-maintained budget hotel than institutional ward. I had a private room over-looking a courtyard. There was a flat-screen TV, a soft-hued impressionist print, and wood-effect laminate flooring. Each day, an orderly brought D and me tea and biscuits, and each night the nurse wrote a note to the janitor so he wouldn't throw away my newspapers and magazines.

The doctor who rigged me up with needles and tubes was a newly arrived Romanian named Elian who practiced his English idioms on me. I was happy for the distraction from the vials of blood he was draining from my arm, except for the time on day three when he tried to make a joke about having to take more blood and I didn't get it was a joke. Both Elian and the nurses seemed fascinated by my treatment, which I later learned was because the hospital was mostly occupied by elective plastic-surgery patients. My treatment for a "real" problem made me something of a medical curiosity.

The day after my treatment ended, I awoke at home to find my bedroom window framing coal-sized blobs of moss plunging to the ground. It was a violent change from the normal tree with field tableau. For a moment I thought these were the world's first suicidal plants, then I realized it was a blackbird violently shifting them from the places on the roof slates where they had nested all winter. It was officially spring, and I guess it was time for these blobs to make a nest for someone else.

For the next two weeks, I spent a lot of time looking out that bedroom window as I lay recuperating from the aftereffects of the steroids, which was in some ways more debilitating, if less scary, than the symptoms. It is a view at which I could gaze indefinitely. The twelve windowpanes, whose frames are badly in need of a paint job, look out over a high stone wall and house behind ours, an ancient horse-chestnut tree, and beyond, St. George's field, which slopes up into a horizon of green, tree-lined hills. After a week, I went to see the neurologist again, who seemed as pleased at my progress as he was stoic and scary when he first saw me weeks before. He prescribed one more week of looking out the window, followed by a cautiously optimistic game of wait and see.

The Grand National

THE UK IS IN LOVE with horse racing, so much so that there are betting tips every day on BBC Radio 4's flagship morning news program, *Today,* roughly the equivalent of NPR's *Morning Edition.* Another regular segment on this show is Thought of the Day, in which a priest or rabbi or imam offers some spiritual insight in the form of a quickie sermon. That these two segments sit alongside each other without any trace of either irony or discomfort is perhaps the best illustration I can offer of the difference between America and the UK.

My first outing following the treatment was to the wine bar to watch my favorite horse race of the year, The Grand National. Miles was working behind the bar, and his reliable reply to my inquiry of how he was—"marvelous now that you are here"—made me feel particularly good that day. He just happens to have a bookkeeper who is also a bookmaker, and so the small group that had assembled was able to call in some bets before the race began. (Between this and the wine, free-range eggs, and homemade marmalade on offer, this place was getting dangerously close to supplying all my needs in life.) I broke my cardinal rule of choosing my bets based on horse's names I like, instead opting for two tips I read in the appropriately named "How to Spend It" supplement in the weekend *Financial Times.* This is how I came to have Snowy Morning and Butler's Cabin to win.

At 4:20 PM, the race got underway in a manner befitting of the Mr. Toad's Wild Ride of horse racing. There are no starting stalls in The Grand National. Instead the forty competing horses just rushed the starting line like a school of crazed fish. There were two false starts before the official let them get under way on the four-and-a-half-mile course.

The other distinctive feature of The Grand National is the fences, thirty of them to be exact. They look like giant hedgerows, taller than the horses, some with ditches and water features and names like The Chair and Becher's Brook. Surviving the process of elimination—which is as much what winning this race is about as being fast—starts at the first jump when a handful of horses or their jockeys or both go down. This continues over every jump, and it is a dramatic, sometimes wrenching sight with horses lolling on their backs and jockeys in a protective, head-clutching fetal position as they try to avoid impact from other horses flying over the fences behind them. A handful of jockeyless horses still make their way around the course at any point in the race, oblivious to the fact that they're disqualified and generally posing a hazard to everyone else. None of my horses won, but it was no small feat that all three finished. Only seventeen of the forty did.

The finish line was not the only milestone reached that afternoon. After three straight weeks of being patient and solemn and an emotional rock, D finally relaxed enough to start introducing some humor into my recent health scare. He joked with Miles about how it would go down in our small rural community if he left me now that I was a "disabled lady." Miles replied it would depend on how fast and with whom I then took up, a scenario that, judging by D's expression, he had failed to consider. Both Miles and Roddy had been a comfort since the whole MS scare had begun. Roddy had confided his own daughter had MS, somewhat demystifying the disease in the process, and Miles had sprung into action, tapping into his network to get advice on the best neurologists in the region. And now, right on cue, Miles was also ready with a bit of deadpan humor.

The joking was a relief to me. Ever since the possibility of MS surfaced, I had been concerned about the impact to D's depression. But instead of sinking him into one, the experience had the opposite effect. He had been calm and devoted throughout. Although he was dealing with the same terrifying thoughts about the potential impact of this disease that I was, it was as if his subconscious wouldn't allow him to melt down. We were part of a team, and two of us couldn't be on the bench at the same time.

I was feeling great but cautious, having made the mistake of spending an hour that morning on WebMD reading up on MS after showing such exquisite restraint with Internet research earlier in my treatment. It was filled with depressing articles called things like "MS and Your Career" or "MS and Intimacy." The thing that got me most about my prognosis was the uncertainty. Even if I was diagnosed, it didn't offer much more insight into what happened next. The symptoms I could experience ranged from a little muscle spasticity or feeling like my foot is asleep to loss of bladder control, sudden paralysis, or blindness at intervals of anything from weeks to months to years between episodes. I must have been at that stage in confronting bad news where you try to find meaning in things, because the parallels to the Grand National seemed obvious. First there was the rapid-fire process of elimination that got me to my initial diagnosis: voice-box damage, stroke, and brain tumor knocked out in consecutive days like horses fallen at consecutive gates. And like MS, the odds mean little in The Grand National. The winner, Mon Mome, was one hundred to one, while another favorite, Hear the Echo, collapsed and died in the run in. I took comfort in Butler's Cabin, one of my bets, who finished in seventh but collapsed shortly after crossing the finish line. He was quickly revived by a dose of oxygen, springing to his feet to the relieved cheers of the crowd.

Les Ions

THE REST OF SPRING was spent adjusting to the new reality of living in the not knowing. (Of course all of life is living in the not knowing, it's just that most of mine I've been lucky enough to maintain the delusion of knowing afforded by the luck of birth, relatively stable employment and relationships, and material comfort.) D and I both thought and spoke of the "what if" daily. I monitored every physiological tick with the vigilance of a sniper. No cramp or tingle went unconsidered, and when I confused a consonant or dropped a syllable, D always asked, half-joking, if I had MS.

In June my right arm started to feel weak. I noticed it most when I was driving and draped it on the armrest or laid it in my lap in an imaginary sling position to get relief. I was worried it was an MS-related symptom, but D was convinced it was nothing. He told me I was just getting older and feeling creaky is to be expected. The problem was that he's understandably invested in my not exhibiting MS symptoms, having no desire to ponder a future in which he gets to play nursemaid to someone with a chronic illness. The part of me that knows positive thinking matters in situations like these welcomed his optimism. But another part of me knew he was a fundamentally unreliable narrator on this subject.

The real question was how much I could rely on my own judgment. It was as if 24/7 surveillance has been installed in my central nervous system, but I didn't yet know if I could trust the person monitoring it. Was it an Agent Scully type in charge, smart and grounded even in the face of an alien attack on my neurons? Or was it just an overzealous mall cop on duty, stirring up symptoms to justify his own inflated sense of self-importance?

One day, my inner mall cop somehow got ahold of my neurologist's phone number and asked if we could come in early, a few weeks ahead of my three-month follow-up appointment, already scheduled for the end of the month. My neurologist was on vacation. The receptionist asked if I would like to be referred to a colleague, at which point Scully took over and said it would not be necessary. And so I waited another two weeks with a low-grade feeling of apprehension resident in my gut. It was as if I have been on a date with MS, and now I was left waiting to see if he was going to call back. Of course I wasn't interested in a second date, but still the days waiting passed in half time, the same for this object of dread as an object of the most intense teenage desire.

My three-month checkup with the neurologist finally arrived. I was still not used to saying I had a neurologist. It's like when you first get married and it feels wildly foreign to refer out loud to your husband. But the strangeness came with a hint of pride. I would rather have a neurologist than, say, a proctologist or a podiatrist. It somehow felt more glamorous, more highbrow, more befitting of me. The corporeal mutiny of age inches forward—an extra chin here, an autoimmune attack there—but that one vestige of youth, my vanity, remains.

The checkup was more of a check-in. In fact, my neurologist would make a great shrink. He has mastered the therapist's technique whereby the patient poses a burning question and the therapist manages to get the patient to answer it through a deft combination of silence and answering a question with another question. The burning question of this appointment was what to do next: nothing or scan again? The latter option meant I would be actively searching for evidence of new "activity" in the brain despite a lack of symptoms. (Within the first two minutes of my appointment the doctor dismissed the lazy arm that earlier in the

month caused me a spasm of panic; it was not an MS symptom.)
If the scan revealed symptom-free activity, it was enough to get
me an MS diagnosis, which is the trigger to start on medication.
American doctors are generally promedicine, so odds are if I was
in the United States, a doctor would advocate a scan. The British
opt for a wait-and-see approach at this stage. And in this matter,
I sided with the country in which I had just become a citizen. I
wanted to enjoy the symptom-free life I was experiencing for as
long as it lasted, hopefully the next sixty years or so.

I knew this was my decision before I walked into the doctor's
office, but I still subjected him to a thirty-minute interrogation.
I was desperate for my symptom-free three months to mean
something of statistical significance about reducing my chances
of developing MS. They did not. They meant what they meant,
which is that I had gone three months without any symptoms.

And that was a good thing.

And that was all.

Still it would have been nice if there was some sort of ceremony
to present me with a three months' symptom-free Alcoholics
Anonymous–style token, something I could carry around in my
pocket and finger inconspicuously when I was feeling insecure.
Instead I got a Zen koan of not knowing to mull over indefinitely.

There were, however, a few pieces of new information I
gleaned from my questioning. The first was that more instances
of MS occur the farther away from the equator you go in either
direction. My neurologist slipped this into a response to a question I had about treatment in the United States versus the UK,
citing the equator effect in explanation for why he couldn't give
me an accurate answer.

"I'm sorry, I don't know what you mean," I said, concerned that
he was really a quack witch-doctor masquerading as a neurologist.

What was he going to say next? Cats can suck the air out of
babies' mouths? But instead he went on to explain the epidemiolog-
ical phenomenon of MS and the equator, which I later confirmed
on the Internet, a validation process that undoubtedly sends

shudders up the spine of every doctor in the land. Unfortunately the relationship is not causal, which meant there was no excuse to pack up and move to the Caribbean just yet.

The second piece of news was that those three sessions of intensive steroid treatments I did back in March only treated my symptoms, the brain swelling that subsequently caused me difficulty speaking. They did nothing to address the underlying cause, a series of lesions on my brain. In fact, the aftermath of these lesions will always be with me. Should I ever have want or need for another brain scan, I will first be shot full of dye so the doctor can tell any new lesions from the old. This was information that did not square well with my core belief system that you are generally in control of your life. Surely there was something I could do to rid myself of these lesions, some combination of oily fish and pomegranates and yoga, if no miracle drug was yet available, as my neurologist told me was the case.

It reminded me of an experience the previous year when I went to see a ballet at the Royal Opera House. My seat was in a box just off stage left, from where I could peer directly down into the orchestra pit. I don't remember much about the ballet, *La Sylphide,* I think, but I do remember looking down at the conductor and thinking with some sadness that I was probably too old to ever be able to do that. By which I meant, at thirty-six, it was unrealistic to think I could ever become an orchestra conductor. Not that I ever aspired to be an orchestra conductor, or a musician of any sort. I terminated my music career at will upon graduating from the eighth grade—everyone knows high school marching band is for losers—having scaled the heights of third-chair flute in the Fort Myers Middle School band. But in that moment at the opera house, I sensed the realm of all of life's possibility slipping away just a bit as I came to grips with the middleness of both my age and my life's achievements. It would almost be tragic, if it wasn't so narcissistic.

Of course, I blame my parents for this obscene level of self-belief and sense of control over my own destiny that allowed me to think well into my thirties I might be capable of one day usurping Sir Simon Rattle if I just tried hard enough. They have always thought I am smarter than I am. (My father still thinks if I would have taken my SATs one more time I could have breached the Ivy wall instead of settling for my respectable yet second-tier university). I suppose this life philosophy has served me well despite the inherent dose of denial. But it also explains why I was having so much trouble coping with the information that there was nothing I could do to rig the odds with this disease.

In the absence of any answers from science I turned to the transformative power of language. Lesions were for lepers or people with venereal disease. They simply would not do. Therefore, I decided I had *les ions,* pronounced lā-ē-uh, with a trademark French grunt on the last syllable. It still sounded vaguely scientific, yet at the same time foreign and alluring. And best of all, it made me feel, just for a moment, like I was in control.

There was in all of this, a parallel to D's depression, which came in handy for empathizing with him in those moments of blackness when he was not the relatively inoffensive-marathon-television watcher but rather the lashing-out lout. (Yes, despite the initial remission, as more time went by without further neurological symptoms in me, his mistress started to make the occasional appearance.) Like les ions, D's depression was largely out of his control. And like les ions, D's depression would likely always be there, an uninvited but recurring guest. Now I knew firsthand the feeling of terror when that uninvited guest first appears at your door. It was a sort of tragicomic quid pro quo: I was learning how to better live with his erratic mistress, and now he was going to have to learn to live with mine.

There was one final thing the neurologist told us on that three-month check-in. While there was nothing I could do to get rid of les ions, there was something I could do to lessen my chances of developing full-blown MS. He mentioned it almost as a throwaway, somewhere between the equator and the les ions: "There was a recent study that gave some indication a pregnancy could help."

I sat gaping, wondering if D was thinking what I was thinking: Did the doctor really just say that, and did my mother put him up to it? I was so stunned, I barely heard him mention a study that showed comparable results from increasing your intake of diet sodas.

Ever since the threat of MS had appeared, I had been avoiding any further consideration of having a child. Until now, I had thought there was some logic to this, as the medicine I would need to take if diagnosed shouldn't be taken if you are pregnant. Amidst all the confusion and upset when the neurologist first explained what was wrong with me, this was the one silver lining. I could put my decision about children, already on ice, into deep freeze. D was understandably too preoccupied with what the potential diagnosis would mean for our lives to pursue the topic. Even my parents didn't have the nerve to ask me about it under the circumstances. Now, with thirteen words, all that had changed.

This Little Piggy
Went to Market

T HROUGHOUT THIS TIME our friends were generous in helping to distract me from the prospect of MS. In the spring Jonny, the shepherd, had taken us to market, specifically the Worcester sale of two hundred store cattle, one stud bull, and eight hundred store sheep, plus calves and weanlings.

The first challenge was deciding what to wear. D and I were both very excited about the prospect of our authentic rural outing and on the morning of, we discussed our outfits like no outfit I had discussed since readying myself for a Friday night at Skatetown USA circa 1983. He settled on his checked shirt, a red tie, and gray sweater vest with jeans and wellies. I chose my suede-elbowed turtleneck sweater, jeans, Chelsea boots, and a flat cap. I decided bringing a purse just wasn't the thing to do at a livestock auction so I carried my things in the pocket of my moth-eaten Burberry wax coat. Luckily said pocket was designed to hold a game bird so it had no problem with my phone and wallet, which is the closest thing to a pheasant it's ever likely to see.

At 8:30 AM, we arrived, as instructed, at a farm just outside Stow-on-the-Wold. Jonny texted that he was still busy loading up the lambs he was taking to market, so we had a poke around while we waited. There were some kennels and a roaming herd of chickens, including a handsome hen of marbled black and white who seemed distressed by my attempts to take a picture of her

with my cell phone. Thankfully the Gloucester Old Spot was
very amenable to the distraction of some wannabe country
folks eager to pat her snout. She was so cute, I thought about
swearing off pork. That lasted as long as it took to drive to the
market and discover there was a canteen and enough time for a
bacon buttie and cup of tea before the auction began.

Before breakfast, we had watched as the lambs from Jonny's
farm and others were unloaded into sheltered pens. Once the
unloading was done, an elaborate sorting process began to get
sheep of similar shapes and sizes grouped together for sale. It
looked like chaos, with pens opening and closing at seemingly
random intervals and a man in a blue jumpsuit making a noise
somewhere between a whistle and a hiss while waving his arms
like he was directing a 747 onto the taxiway. I tried to stay out
of the way while Jonny got into the pens and helped herd errant
sheep. I figured D and I had already embarrassed him enough
by having our picture taken dipping our boots in the buckets of
antiseptic by every door.

When the auction bell rang at 10:30 AM, we headed outside
and joined the sea of flat caps. The auctioneer, a youngish, bet-
ter-looking version of Prince Harry dressed in a checked shirt,
tie, and white lab coat, stepped up on the concrete wall that
ran the length of the pens and started the bidding. Jonny had
warned me not to wink, nod, or twitch while they were selling.
It didn't take long to figure out why. Bidding seemed to be done
by a mere widening of the eyes or a pocket-encased finger wag.
When the first lot went for £42, I was shocked at how cheap
sheep were and felt an irrational itch to bid. I started to hatch
plans to rent some land and form a wine-bar/sheep syndicate.
Then Jonny explained that was the price per sheep, not as I
had thought for the entire pen. As we walked from pen to pen
following the auctioneer, Jonny also explained the difference
between a Texel and a Suffolk Cross and why his farm opts for
an unhandsome French breed called Charolais: Small heads
and big bodies means easy lambing and good meat. He also

answered a thousand and one other questions we had that were the farming equivalent of a six-year-old asking his father why the sky is blue. In addition to D asking Jonny if his outfit was all right ("Your flat cap is too new" was the reply), these questions included what store lambs and store cattle mean, which is that these animals were being sold off to continue to be raised on other farms rather than destined straight for the abattoir. In the end, this would be their fate, but knowing this wasn't imminent made the proceedings jollier.

After the sheep were sold, we all headed into a sort of miniature amphitheater for the cattle auction. There were plywood-step bleachers, but most people stood on the cold dirt floor facing a half moon-shaped pen. The auctioneer, a different, older man this time, stood with a portable microphone in a booth behind the pen. The star of the show was the stud bull, a Pingauzer named Elgany John Jack. From the program notes, I knew his mother's name was Our Wilma and his father Edenbrook Cassius. I also knew that our stud bull never knew his father as Our Wilma was serviced by Edenbrook Cassius via the medium of imported Austrian semen. Perhaps it was rage over his absentee father that made it sound like King Kong rattling the bars of his cage when Elgany John Jack stepped onto the weighing pen scales. But when this ginger-colored beast entered the viewing arena, I couldn't help thinking he had a touch of Liberace about him. It was the combination of his mop of curls poised on his head like a too small toupee, the golden ring through his nose, and the way his hooves made him walk like he was wearing a pair of Manolos. In the end he went for substantially more than a pair of Manolos.

We ended the morning with a coffee in the market canteen. There, seated with a few other shepherds, talk turned to lambing, which was starting soon at Jonny's farm. I learned that snow is not of much concern during lambing but rain is, that you rarely need to assist a ewe in giving birth (despite what I had seen on all those episodes of *All Creatures Great and Small*), and that the whole thing lasts the better part of two weeks. I had wangled my invitation before we left.

A few weeks later we were back at Jonny's farm for lambing. About six hundred of the farm's seven hundred sheep had already given birth, so Jonny must have figured that at this point D and I could inflict minimal damage. Heeding his advice, I dressed sensibly in jeans and a sweatshirt. D, on the other hand, had found it unnecessary to change out of the tweed blazer and cravat—his latest rural accessory—he had worn to church; wellies were his sole sartorial concession.

Not long after we arrived, I spotted a ewe that was about to give birth. I won't describe here how I could tell she was about to give birth, only that it involved some telltale signs visible from the rear and that unlike Alice, the shepherdess on duty with Jonny, I couldn't sit around slurping an instant pot noodle while I watched said signs expand, contract, and leak. Waiting for this ewe to give birth was like waiting for a watched pot to boil, so we strolled around the individual pens that had been set up for ewes and their new babies on the other side of the barn. One pen looked like a dismantled kids' playhouse with daisies painted on the side and a heat lamp hanging overhead. Inside, five lambs were regularly reassembling themselves from huddle to snoozing heap. These five were too small to make it on their own when they were born so they were being hand-reared as pets. This included feeding them what looked like orange Gatorade through a syringe while the no-nonsense Alice held them upright by their front legs. The cutest was a girl called Jeff with a black face and black legs. She was already so domesticated, she cuddled like a kitten.

Back in the lambing pens, the expectant ewes were looking fed up. There was a lot of panting and pawing going on, and it was hard not to anthropomorphize these ewes when the look of disgust in their eyes was so similar to that I had seen in women in labor on television. This experience was certainly doing nothing to encourage me to get pregnant. Of course, I had been thinking more about what the neurologist told me at my recent appointment, and I couldn't shake the idea that getting pregnant because it might lessen my chances of developing a disease that might or might not be debilitating if I got it was somehow a little perverse. As a solution, it seemed at best drastic and at worst teetering on the edge of unethical. D had given me a wide berth on this one, saying, as always, the decision was up to me.

At the moment, he was preoccupied having spotted another ewe who had started to give birth. (Ewe number one was still holding out.) Within five minutes, a tiny, gooey lamb had plopped out on the straw. The mother was immediately upright, licking and preening, and the other ewes gave her space. Within five more minutes, the lamb was taking her first steps, just in time for her mother to lie down again. Out came a twin, another girl, which took even less time than the first.

At this point, D had already named the lambs Lord and Lady Glebe, never mind they were both girls, and was asking to buy them at well over market prices. He even offered to go into town right then to get cash out of the ATM. He didn't want to take them home to our pebble courtyard, just to buy them a life as replacement stock rather than heading to the abattoir in as soon as twelve weeks. I was trying to be more sensible and embrace the "know where your food comes from" ethic, so suggested we should buy them to eat. We could, I wanted to think, enjoy eating them knowing that they were reared and killed ethically. But the truth is I don't think any of us, except Alice of course, could have eaten Lord and Lady Glebe after we spent a few more minutes watching them come to life like those sponge toys that metamorphose from a cubic centimeter to an animal when you sprinkle them with water.

Jonny explained that in the next few days Lord and Lady G would get a number spray painted on their side, the same as their mother, to make sure they all end up together when they are put out to pasture. He promised to make note of their numbers and keep an eye on them so he could report back to us on their progress. He said there was a good chance they would end up as replacement breeding stock anyway—their mother gave birth to twins, which means they have hearty breeding genes. The odds seemed no worse than my own for developing MS, so I was happy to believe it was true.

The Game Fair

Rupert and Ralph pitched in with the entertainment during the summer when they took D and me to a game fair. That's game as in pheasant and grouse, not Scrabble and Monopoly. And yes, I knew that before I attended. I even offered to drive, but Rupert and Ralph deemed arriving at the game fair in my Toyota Prius unacceptable.

"We'll take the E-class," Rupert sniffed.

We also took their Norfolk terrier, Teddy, terriers being de rigueur at this sort of thing. There was, in fact, a large swathe of activity dedicated to dogs, including dog shows, hunting hounds, vets, and people hawking pet insurance. Held on the grounds of a stately home, the show amounted to a mass outdoor mall dedicated to all things associated with the British countryside, not just dogs but also guns (as with dogs, guests were free to enter with their own) and fishing and falconry. There were also people selling teak tiki huts for outdoor dining, Airstream trailers (a rare American incursion along with the bring-your-gun mentality), and every piece of clothing imaginable rendered in tweed. Guests were free to make use of the helicopter landing pad, an indicator of the target demographic and perhaps at least a partial explanation of why a £21 per person entrance fee was no deterrent to the crowds. As Rupert observed, "What recession?"

We started our tour of the fair with a sharpener at the Pimms and champagne tent, followed by a photo op milking a plastic cow and a hog roast and cider lunch. We then headed for Gunmakers' Row where I was immediately taken with a ladies' sporting ensemble of raspberry-velvet waistcoat with pale blue silk cravat and delicate tweed plus-fours. It was enough to make me give away all my personal details to *Shooting Gazette,* "Driven Shooting's Finest Journal," for a chance to win £1,000 worth of shooting clothes. The nice gentleman also gave me a copy of the July issue, which featured articles such as "10 Steps to Being the Perfect Gun: How to Avoid Embarrassment and Be a First-Class Guest" and "Confused by Cartridges? The Questions You Never Dared Ask." It made amusing bathtub reading.

Ralph, the only real shooter amongst our group, accompanied me into the tent of the gunmakers Holland and Holland, which looked like something in which you might take gin-based cocktails while on a luxury safari. As we browsed, he explained in hushed tones that guns here are sold in pairs so your loader—the shooting equivalent of a caddy—can be readying one while you are shooting the other. Prices went as high as £100,000 per gun. Luckily I was more interested in a fetching silk scarf with knotted fringe ends and a pattern of forest creatures reminiscent of medieval French tapestry.

"Don't hesitate," a cravated man stage-whispered to me in Italian-accented English. "They're going fast."

The hard sell took me by surprise, and instead of the scarf I opted for buying a round of ice cream cones for the group, which we ate while admiring the local human wildlife. Even though it was the middle of summer, the look for women under thirty was knee-high brown boots, a skintight tweed miniskirt, a tailored long-sleeved shirt in pink or stripes—the kind I might wear with a suit—and a mane of long, straight hair. The options for men seemed more varied, and my favorite was the lederhosen-evoking, velvet Bermuda shorts sported by a fellow customer in the Holland and Holland enclosure. He had both the height and the überposh accent to carry off the look.

We ended the day with D and Ralph taking in a round of target practice on the shooting range. I didn't join in. Despite my admiration for the accoutrements of shooting, I was feeling particularly aimless. Little did I know that was all about to change.

The Not-So-Simple Life

AUGUST IN THE COTSWOLDS is harvest time. Just on the outskirts of town, a corn dryer rumbled away, blanketing the countryside in a backdrop of white noise. Those stalks of grain still left in the fields were bleached the exact color of the dry stone walls that enclosed them. In the already harvested fields, giant Swiss rolls of hay sat patiently alongside flocks of displaced seagulls. Spiky crystal balls crowned by smaller fuchsia bulbs dotted the hedgerows, Venetian glass ornaments masquerading as thistles.

August also marked the passage of six months since the discovery of les ions on my brain, with no further recurrence of symptoms. In the first few months, I had felt like a woman who is engaged, and all of a sudden it seems to her as if the entire world is getting married. MS was all around me. There was the morning news story about a woman with chronic MS who was testing a legal case for the right to assisted suicide at the Swiss clinic, Dignitas. Or that time the middle-aged couple sat down next to me in a café and struck up a conversation. The man was in a wheelchair and, apropos of nothing, the woman told me MS was to blame. Then, once at a party, an acquaintance mentioned she was just back from visiting her brother, who is now bedridden from MS. Each time this happened, my physiological reaction was the same. My breathing shallowed. My insides constricted, amplifying my awareness of the corridor running from gut to nose. I felt still and quiet and small, even though outwardly I was listening and nodding.

But now, six months on, my interest in MS had started to wane, and in the preceding month I had thought of it very little. It's not so much that I had learned to live with the not knowing, more like I became expert in how to avoid it, much like the question of motherhood.

Toward the end of August I flew to Boston for work, where I was to meet with a particular executive for the first time. We sat in his corner office, his chubby face peering out at me over his desk as he slow-burned through a series of roundabout questions, culminating in whether or not I was "in a good place in my life" to take on more work. It dawned on me that this was the politically correct way a white American male asked a woman in her late thirties if it was safe to promote her. Was she preoccupied by young children? Was she planning on announcing a pregnancy anytime soon? These were the questions that shimmered just under the surface of our chatter. My response, which felt like an awkward confessional, came without hesitation: Yes, I was in a good place.

It was a relief. For one thing, it proved to me I'd reached a milestone in my perception about the prospect of developing MS. I knew I was still at risk, but enough time had passed that the threat was no longer hovering over my psyche, exerting undeserved influence on my choices. The executive was thinking of kids, not chronic disease, and I was clearly thinking of neither. I had answered like I always hoped I would answer a koan back in my Zen practitioner days in Los Angeles: without a second thought. Finally, when I least expected it, I had admitted to not wanting kids.

When I got home and told D, he was also relieved, mostly that I had finally made a decision about having children in which he felt he could have some confidence. Thinking back on our last meeting with the neurologist, we recalled that his tone sounded tenuous when describing both the study that indicated pregnancy might help prevent MS and the study that suggested the active ingredient in diet sodas might do the same. We both agreed that drinking a Diet Coke a day seemed the far less radical of the two options.

And so that night we celebrated with a dinner of Kung Pao chicken from the Chinese takeout restaurant. As we ate, we reminisced about the last year and a half and realized how miserably we had failed to fulfill the unspoken promise of life in the country: the simple life. Aside from acquiring a new vocabulary of dogs and foxes and horses and guns, and tweed and waterproof clothing for doing things with dogs and foxes and horses and guns, very little had actually changed. Sure, I fantasized about converting the post office to a tea shop, selling the kind of gifts women give other women. But in the end, I had nodded my head *yes* in that Boston executive's office.

Life in the country didn't do much to simplify D's existence either. Commuting between London and bliss just meant that the availability of bliss threw the inhumanity of urban life into sharp relief. And he has found that while long walks in the countryside are palliative, they are still no cure for depression. Combined with cognitive behavioral therapy, however, they are the best treatment we know.

In the end, the countryside didn't change us. It just made us more of who we already were. And so, Diet Coke in hand, we toasted our family of four—D, the mistress, les ions, and me—living the not-so-simple life.

Field Guide Number Four:

Walk for appreciating the not-so-simple life

HAMPNETT

Monarch's Way

A429

Wine Bar

Church of
St. Peter & St. Paul
All Alone

X Start &
Finish
Here

NORTHLEACH

Distance	4 miles (approximately)
Duration	1.5 hours
Difficulty	Easy, a perfect walk for when you are feeling fragile

A short loop from Northleach to the sleepy hamlet of Hampnett and back, this was the first walk I did after recuperating from my steroid treatment. It is gentle and rewarding, a perfect walk for when you are feeling fragile.

1. Head out All Alone, the same way as you did on the Gay Pumpkin Walk, or, for a more scenic route, follow the path out of the graveyard behind the Church of Saint Peter and Saint Paul. Just cross the stream and head up the hill where you will join All Alone.

2. Take care crossing the busy A429 and continue up the lane. At the first crossroads go right. Shortly thereafter, you will see a path on your right signposted MONARCH'S WAY. Follow the path along the field until you reach the road.

3. Cross straight over the road and go around the gate, continuing straight on the path downhill. You should have a nice view of Hampnett in front of you now, including herds of contented caramel-colored cows.

4. At the bottom of the hill, head right along the path, curving around uphill until you are at the main lane through the hamlet. Stop and sit a while on the bench in front of the church, where you can admire the Tudor barn conversion across the street and are likely to be paid a visit by a friendly ginger tom.

5. If you are feeling curious, you can head right (from sitting on the bench; left if facing the church) and explore the rest of the hamlet via the main road. If not, just head left along the lane until you get to the main road, the A429 again. Turn right and head downhill on the sidewalk, then left at the traffic lights into Northleach.

6. At Antelope Cottage you can turn right and follow the path back up to the church, or, if you are in need of refreshment, continue on to the wine bar in the market square. A gathering of lovable eccentrics clad in corduroy and tweed awaits your arrival.

Acknowledgments

THANK YOU to my early readers and editors: Michael, Suzanna, Samantha, and Aimée. Aimée, you cannot ask for more in an older sister than a teen-aged introduction to Joan Didion and *The New Yorker*. Suzanna, you have been a creative force in my life since our days of tap dancing in the kitchen. Michael, I look forward to a childfree retirement where we vacation together and behave inappropriately for our age.

Thank you to my parents, who always did and still do think I am capable of doing anything, even if they hoped for something different than writing a book where I poke fun at them.

And finally, thanks to my husband, that self-appointed muse without whom there would be far less to write about.

About the Author

© Karl Larsen

Jennifer Richardson is an American Anglophile who spent three years living in a Cotswold village populated straight out of English central casting by fumbling aristocrats, gentlemen farmers, and a village idiot. She is married to an Englishman who, although not the village idiot, provides her with ample writing material. She currently lives in Santa Monica, California along with her husband and her royal wedding tea towel collection.

You can find Jennifer online at:
www.americashire.com
www.twitter.com/baronessbarren
www.facebook.com/americashire
www.pinterest.com/baronessbarren